EXAM *Revision* S

AQA AS
Business Studies

Malcolm Surridge

Philip Allan Updates, an imprint of Hodder Education, an Hachette UK company, Market Place, Deddington, Oxfordshire OX15 0SE

Orders

Bookpoint Ltd, 130 Milton Park, Abingdon, Oxfordshire OX14 4SB
tel: 01235 827720
fax: 01235 400454
e-mail: uk.orders@bookpoint.co.uk

Lines are open 9.00 a.m.–5.00 p.m., Monday to Saturday, with a 24-hour message answering service. You can also order through the Philip Allan Updates website:
www.philipallan.co.uk

© Philip Allan Updates 2009

ISBN 978-0-340-95855-1

First printed 2009
Impression number   5   4   3   2
Year   2014   2013   2012   2011   2010   2009

All web addresses included in the book are correct at the time of going to press but may subsequently change.

Printed in Spain

Environmental information
Hachette UK's policy is to use papers that are natural, renewable and recyclable products and made from wood grown in sustainable forests. The logging and manufacturing processes are expected to conform to the environmental regulations of the country of origin.

P01391

AQA AS Business Studies

Contents

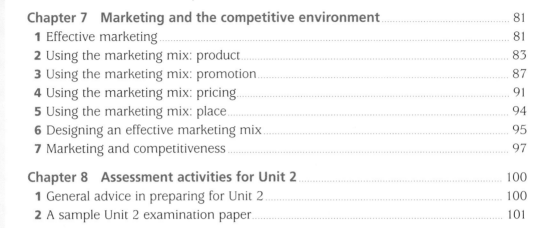

Introduction

About this book

This book of revision notes is intended to form a central part of your revision programme. Read this introduction carefully before you attempt to use the notes that follow. It contains some important advice that is intended to help you improve your performance and final grade.

The notes cover all the important subject matter that may be taught as part of the AQA AS Business Studies course. The content and the examination advice have been fully revised to take into account the changes introduced in 2008. Thus you can use the book with confidence.

The book is divided into two sections to cover Unit 1 and Unit 2 of the AQA AS Business Studies specification. Each section is divided into chapters that fit precisely with the AQA specification. In turn, each of these chapters is divided into topics that follow the AQA specification exactly. So, by working your way through this book, you can be confident that you have covered the specification.

Make sure you are clear which sections of the book relate to the topics you are studying at any given time, and work through the relevant chapter. This will:
- identify any material that you may not have covered
- reinforce your initial learning
- provide a sound basis for revision prior to the examination(s)

Within the text, important terms are put in **bold** to attract your attention. Finally, the 'Examiner's tips' throughout these notes are special pieces of advice written to help you to understand both the subject and how best to approach it.

The AQA AS Business Studies course

The structure of the course

The AS qualification has two units of study:
- **Unit 1: Planning and financing a business.** This unit covers the range of activities involved in starting a new business and is designed to introduce you to the subject. It covers the breadth of business studies but does not look at any topics in depth — this comes later in the course. Unit 1 considers the qualities that successful entrepreneurs require as well as what motivates entrepreneurs to take the risk of starting a business. The unit considers all of the information that is required in a business plan, including financial information. Finally, it encourages you to reflect on the quality of business planning and to consider what represents good-quality planning.
- **Unit 2: Managing a business.** Unit 2 looks at the four internal functions of a business that managers have to control. These are finance, marketing, operations management and managing people or human resources. The unit considers how managers might measure the performance of the business in each of these functional areas and how the performance of each function may be improved. The unit also introduces you to the competitive environment in which businesses operate. You will be expected to know what makes a business competitive and how managers can improve the competitiveness of their organisations.

The AS 'story'

There is a story running through the AQA AS Business Studies specification which is continued when you study the subject at A2. Understanding the story will help you to study the subject effectively and to tackle the examinations successfully.

The story starts in Unit 1 with the planning of a business. The central point about this unit of study is that it focuses on the business *before* it starts trading. Therefore this unit is about small-scale businesses trading in local markets or possibly throughout the UK. The key theme is planning the business. To play a part in the story, you could cast yourself in the role of an entrepreneur who is establishing a business and is looking forward to the time when the business is actively trading. The story at this pre-trading stage considers all the aspects of planning a new enterprise that are necessary to give it the best chance of success. At this stage the story introduces you to marketing, finance, managing people and operations, but all within the context of planning a new business. You should consider the quality of the planning that is taking place and think about the strengths and weaknesses in the process.

Unit 2 takes the story forward a stage. It assumes that the planning is complete and that the business has started trading — indeed, it may have been trading for a number of years. Thus, in this unit the story progresses to consider small and medium-sized businesses that may be selling locally, regionally or throughout the UK. At this stage of the story, you become the manager of a business and you are seeking ways to improve the performance of your business. The story covers a range of tactical (or short-term) actions that you may take to achieve an improvement in the performance of the business. All of these actions are functional, in that they relate to the functions (such as marketing) of the business. So this unit looks at marketing actions or finance-based actions that the managers of small and medium-sized businesses might use to improve the business. Examples include training employees, cutting price, persuading customers to pay sooner and using the business's resources more intensively.

The examinations

The Unit 1 examination

This examination is based on a case study and lasts for 1 hour and 15 minutes. The case study will explain the story of a business start-up. You will have to tackle a series of questions, ranging from simple definitions of business terms worth 2 marks to questions calling for much longer responses. These latter questions will require you to develop arguments and make and support judgements, and they could be worth up to 15 or 16 marks. The total mark allocation for this paper is 60 marks and it carries a 40% weighting for the AS qualification (or 20% for the entire A-level). You can take the Unit 1 examination in January or June.

An example of a Unit 1 examination can be seen in Chapter 3, pages 43–45.

The Unit 2 examination

The Unit 2 examination comprises two data-response questions. Each question has about 250–300 words of text as well as numerical information if appropriate, and four or five questions. These questions all require you to apply your answers to the scenario and most ask you to develop arguments and make judgements. Between them the two questions will cover the four internal functions (finance, marketing, operations management and human resources), although they can be tested in any combination. For example, marketing and finance will not always be tested in the same question.

An example of a Unit 2 examination can be seen in Chapter 8, pages 101–03.

You can find copies of past and specimen AQA AS Business Studies papers on the AQA website at: **www.aqa.org.uk/qual/gce/business_studies_new.php**.

How to revise for AQA AS Business Studies

- **Plan well ahead.** This is the most important thing about preparing for examinations in AS Business Studies.
- **Note down the dates of your examinations.** The AQA GCE Business Studies course has unit examinations, examinations on the individual units comprising the qualification. These unit examinations take place in January and May or June of each year. You will have to take two examinations at AS, and then a further two at A2 to complete the A-level Business Studies course. However, you may choose to re-sit one or more of the unit examinations, so the total number of examinations is likely to be more than four.
- **Make sure you know exactly what material you need to revise for the examination and the style of the examination.** Does the examination take the form of a case study, data-response question(s), an essay, a business report or a combination of these? You should plan a full programme of revision well ahead of any examinations you may be taking.
- **Plan your revision carefully.** If you do not like a section of the specification, make sure you revise it early so that you can iron out any problems — perhaps with help from your teacher or lecturer. He or she will also be able to comment on your revision plans.
- **Look at past papers.** You should have a complete set of past papers. They are invaluable for examination practice. They allow you to see topics that have been examined recently and those not tested for some time. They also enable you to familiarise yourself with the style and level of questions that you will encounter on the day of the examination. Past papers should play a greater role in the later stages of your revision programme. You need to have mastered the subject matter before you start practising past questions. It is also helpful to get hold of copies of at least some of the associated marking schemes. These will allow you to see the sorts of answers that examiners were anticipating to each question and the types of examination skills that you were expected to use.
- **Use these Exam Revision Notes as the centrepiece of your revision.** This book will provide you with all the basic information you require. Don't hesitate to write in the book. Tick off subjects as you feel confident about them. Highlight those topics you find difficult and look at them in detail, using your class notes and textbook to support your study.
- **Make sure that you cover all the topics that may form a part of the examination.** Don't skip topics. Plan your revision programme so that you can work steadily through all the topics in the weeks leading up to the examination. Don't be too ambitious as to how much you can do each week. This means you have to start in plenty of time. This is particularly true if you are revising for several AS examinations in the same sitting.
- **Take any tips on revision techniques from teachers and friends, but do what works for you.** You might find that you remember topics and interrelationships (e.g. the consequences of high gearing) by drawing spider diagrams. On the other hand, you may benefit from completing lots of past papers.

- **Everyone revises differently.** Find out what routine suits you best: alone or with a friend; in the morning or late at night; in short, sharp bursts or in longer revision sessions. Whatever approach you adopt, build in breaks to ensure you remain fresh.
- **Raise any problems or areas of difficulty with your teacher or lecturer**. It is important to eliminate areas of misunderstanding.
- **Attend any revision classes put on by your teacher or lecturer.** Remember, he or she is an expert at preparing people for examinations.

Don'ts

- Don't leave your revision to the last minute.
- Don't avoid revising subjects you dislike or find difficult — in fact, do them first.
- Don't forget that there is a life beyond revision and exams — build leisure and relaxation into your revision programme.
- Don't cram all night before an exam. You would do better to have a night away from revision.

On the day of the examination

- Have a good breakfast.
- Make sure you know where the exam is being held.
- Give yourself plenty of time to get there.
- Take everything you need — extra pens, water, tissues, a watch, Polo mints.
- If you feel anxious, breathe slowly and deeply to help you to relax.

In the examination room

- **Read the instructions at the top of the exam paper and follow them carefully.** A surprising number of students attempt three questions when they have been asked to answer two, for example. Others attempt all the questions, rather than the specified number. Make sure you don't do this.
- **Skim over the paper, identifying the question areas you have revised for.** Spot the questions you can do. Read them carefully.
- **Manage your time carefully.** The examination paper will state the number of marks given for each element of a question. Prior to entering the exam room, you should have worked out how much time you have to answer each part of a question according to the mark allocation — read the examiner's tip below.

Examiner's tip

The best way to manage your time is to calculate the ratio between marks on the paper and the time allocation for the entire paper. This ratio can then be applied throughout the paper, ensuring that you have time to answer all the questions you should.

Example

Suppose your AS Business Studies examination lasts for 90 minutes and the paper is worth 80 marks. If you assume that you will spend 10 minutes reading the paper, this leaves you 80 minutes to plan and write your answers. You therefore have 80 minutes to answer questions worth 80 marks. This means you can afford to spend 1 minute on a question for each mark allocated to it. In these circumstances, you should spend 15 minutes on a 15-mark question and 6 minutes on a 6-mark question.

- **Read through the paper carefully, especially if you have to make a choice of questions.** It is vital that you are clear about what the questions are asking and, if you have to make a choice, that you choose those questions on which you can perform best.
- **Jot down answer plans before you tackle a question.** Only begin writing when you have a clear idea of what the question calls for and your response. Be prepared to amend your answer plan as you develop your answer. Other ideas and information will come to mind as you write; note them in your plan before you forget them.
- **In planning your answers, ensure you know what examination skills are required.** Some questions simply require knowledge; others call for analysis and/or evaluation (see 'Assessment objectives' below). The command word and the mark allocation will tell you what is required.
- **Refer back to the question.** As you write your responses, glance occasionally at the question you are answering. This will help you to write relevantly.
- You may find it reassuring to **attempt your best question first** to settle your nerves. However, do make sure that the questions are not sequential, with the responses to later questions depending on your earlier answers.
- **If you are stuck on a question, go on to the next.** You can always come back to the unfinished one later.
- **Presentation is important.** Set your work out neatly using plenty of paragraphs. A new paragraph is invaluable to indicate a new aspect of the question, or to show that you are using a new examination skill.
- **This also applies to numerical questions.** Set your work out clearly, spacing it out and showing all relevant calculations. Key figures within your answers should be labelled to assist the examiner. In this way, you will receive credit for your work even if you make an arithmetical error.
- **Stay strictly within the time constraints you have calculated.** It is important that you attempt all the questions in order to maximise your marks.
- **Once the examination is over, relax.** Don't brood over any problems in an exam that is completed. It is better to concentrate on the next examination and then to relax when they are all over.
- **Pace yourself during the examination period.** Following a tough examination, a couple of hours spent with friends or watching television will do you more good than a further session of revision.

Assessment objectives

You may ask: 'What are assessment objectives'? They are the skills you require if you are to succeed in AS Business Studies, or any other AS examination for that matter. We have already seen that you will need **understanding** of the subject matter as set out in the specification, but this is not enough for success at AS. You must also have examination skills, such as being able to **apply** your knowledge to the scenario, and to write **analytically** and **evaluatively**. One of the most important formulae to learn for AS is:

AS success = subject knowledge + examination skills

Assessment objectives, or examination skills, in AS Business Studies include:
● knowledge and critical understanding
● application of knowledge to unfamiliar situations
● analysis of problems, issues and situations
● evaluation and synopsis

You will see from this list that knowledge of business studies is only one of a number of skills necessary for success. A critical element of your revision will be to develop these skills. While analysis and evaluation are generally regarded as the key to high grades in AS Business Studies, application is a skill that students find difficulty in mastering. You should try to think about how the theories and concepts that you study relate to different types of business. For example, why might house builders be more vulnerable to cash-flow problems than small retailers? It is important to practise these skills through regular attempts at recent past papers.

Good luck with your revision.

Malcolm Surridge

Unit 1
Planning and financing a business

1 *Enterprise*

What you need to know:

- the meaning of 'enterprise' and 'entrepreneurs'
- the nature of risk and its importance
- the rewards entrepreneurs receive
- how opportunity cost relates to entrepreneurs' decisions
- why people become entrepreneurs
- how the UK government supports entrepreneurs

1.1 Entrepreneurs and enterprise

An **entrepreneur** is a person who is willing to take a risk in starting a new enterprise. Entrepreneurs are important people because, by creating businesses, they provide new jobs and increase the general level of prosperity in the communities in which they operate. Entrepreneurs can be very different. On the one hand, those such as Richard Branson are serial entrepreneurs, creating a succession of businesses and seeing them develop into large-scale organisations. In contrast, it is far more common for entrepreneurs to establish a small business and to continue to manage this business, which may only grow slowly over time, if at all. The high-profile entrepreneurs who appear regularly in the media are the exceptions, not the rule.

Enterprise normally refers to the qualities and talents a person needs to be a successful entrepreneur. Entrepreneurs need a range of abilities if they are to succeed in establishing a business. The Entrepreneurship Forum of New England (**www.efne.org/page/entrepreneur_qualities/**) has identified six key qualities that are found in successful entrepreneurs:

- **dreamer** — having a big idea of how something can be better and different
- **innovator** — demonstrating how the idea applied outperforms current offerings
- **passionate** — being expressive so that the idea creates energy and approval with others
- **risk taker** — pursuing the dream without having all the resources lined up at the start
- **dogged committer** — staying with executing the innovation through the peaks and valleys to make it work
- **continuous learner** — constantly exploring and evolving to do best practice

> *Examiner's tip*
>
> You should look at case studies of real-life entrepreneurs who have set up different types of business. Don't just consider the well-known entrepreneurs; look also for those who operate small businesses and non-profit businesses (or social enterprises).

1.2 Risk and rewards

Risk is the possibility of incurring some misfortune or loss. Entrepreneurs have to learn to live with risk as many new businesses fail. Surveys suggest that between 20% and 30% of new businesses do not survive their first year of trading. If a business fails, it is often the case that the entrepreneur behind it loses some or all of his or her personal wealth. New businesses can fail for a number of reasons:

- There is insufficient demand for the product.
- Competitors respond by taking actions to force a new enterprise out of business.
- The costs of setting up and running the business may be higher than expected.
- The business runs out of cash.

We will look at the reasons behind the failure of new businesses more fully in Chapter 2.

Rewards are those things that an entrepreneur receives in return for taking the risk of starting a new business. The most obvious reward is money. Some entrepreneurs have become very rich. For example, in 2008 Richard Branson's wealth was estimated at £2,700 million. There are other rewards too. These include being one's own boss and not answerable to anyone else, having the satisfaction of creating a business and possibility of passing it onto your children.

1.3 Opportunity cost

Opportunity cost is the next best alternative forgone. In less technical terms, it measures the cost of a decision in terms of what you have to give up as a consequence. Thus the cost for you of a week's holiday in Spain might be the new clothes that you could have bought but cannot afford now.

Entrepreneurs take decisions which can be measured in terms of opportunity cost. The major one is the decision to start the business. Most entrepreneurs give up a job to start a business — the job may be well paid and have substantial perks, such as generous pensions. Other examples of opportunity cost at work are taking on staff (rather than working even longer hours themselves) or borrowing money rather than selling more shares in the company.

Opportunity cost can also help us to make judgements about new businesses. It is possible to evaluate the success of a new business (in financial and non-financial terms) against the income and security that the alternative job provided.

1.4 Motives for becoming an entrepreneur

People decide to start their own businesses for many different reasons. Some of the more common ones are listed below:

- **To become wealthy.** This is a common motivation for starting a business. A small minority of entrepreneurs become very wealthy; many more earn good incomes. Entrepreneurs believe they will receive the full reward for their abilities.
- **Because they have an idea.** Some entrepreneurs have (what they think is) a great idea and believe they can make money out of it. However, it is only a great idea in business terms if it results in a saleable product.
- **Being one's own boss.** For many people the idea of not being answerable to anyone else is attractive. Being able to work flexibly to fit around other commitments is another example of the benefits that entrepreneurship can confer.
- **The satisfaction that results from creativity.** Establishing a new business and seeing it flourish can be highly satisfying. The idea of having a business to pass on to future generations is also very attractive to large numbers of entrepreneurs.

The success of television programmes such as *The Apprentice* and *Dragons' Den* has highlighted the potential rewards from entrepreneurship and may have encouraged many aspiring entrepreneurs to take the plunge.

Ideas for application

Do think about how the motives vary according to the individual and the circumstances. Not all people establish businesses to make money or to become famous. Those setting up social enterprises may have different motivators.

1.5 Government support for enterprise and entrepreneurs

The UK government benefits in many ways from the activities of entrepreneurs. Entrepreneurs create jobs, sometimes in areas with high unemployment. This helps the government to meet its economic target of controlling unemployment and reduces the amount of unemployment benefit it has to pay. Entrepreneurs also pay taxes on their spending and on their business's profits — assuming it makes any. Finally, new businesses can help the general prosperity of an area by, for example, placing orders for goods and services with other businesses, thereby generating further revenues and taxes for the government.

The UK government says that it wants to support entrepreneurs and enterprise 'from classrooms to boardrooms' and this support can take a number of forms:
- **Education.** This entails including enterprise as a topic in the curriculum for all students at school as well as providing subsidised classes for adults.
- **Providing a business-friendly environment.** This means reducing legal barriers to starting a business and limiting the amount of paperwork that is necessary once the business is trading. It also refers to minimising taxes on new businesses.
- **Financial support.** There is a range of government schemes which offer financial support to entrepreneurs. The government guarantees loans made to some small firms (reassuring banks that they will be repaid), provides venture capital to some small and medium-sized businesses and provides additional income for entrepreneurs during the crucial start-up stage of the enterprise's life. The Business Link website provides information on the latest financial support that is available: **www.businesslink.gov.uk/bdotg/action/layer?topicId=1073858790**.
- **Advice and information.** The government seeks to help entrepreneurs deal with the complexities of starting and managing businesses by providing guidance and training. Business Link is a good example of such support.

The government's policies may have been successful, as the number of businesses operating in the UK rose by 750,000 between 1998 and 2008.

2 *Generating and protecting business ideas*

What you need to know:
- the sources of business ideas
- the role and importance of franchises in generating business ideas
- the functions of copyrights, patents and trademarks

2.1 The sources of business ideas

There are a number of ways in which entrepreneurs may generate business ideas:

- **Brainstorming.** This entails a group of people making as many suggestions as possible without attempting to assess them, which can stifle creativity. The ideas are evaluated later.
- **Inventions.** Some but not all inventions can be turned into commercial products. Trevor Bayliss's wind-up radio has become a very successful product in Africa, where mains electricity is not always available.
- **Spotting a gap in the market.** Sometimes a market niche exists which no business is supplying. A **market niche** is a small part of a larger market. However, it may be that the gap exists because it cannot be supplied profitably.
- **Market research.** Entrepreneurs may be conducting market research for one product and inadvertently discover that demand exists for another product. This might be the basis for a highly successful product.

Examiner's tip

Only think about the ways of generating business ideas that are available to small businesses with limited financial resources.

2.2 Purchasing a franchise

A **franchise** is the granting by one business (the **franchisor**) to another individual or business (the **franchisee**) the rights to supply its products. Therefore purchasing a franchise normally means buying a complete business idea from someone else. Franchises are an increasingly common way of starting businesses, especially in the retail sector.

A franchise is a quick way to acquire a business idea and one which has been tested already. The franchisor can offer support and training as well as ongoing advice on operational issues. It may also provide national advertising for the chain of businesses. Buying a franchise reduces (but does not eliminate) the risk of starting a new business.

However, franchises do have distinct disadvantages. Franchisees will have to:

- conform to the business's rules regarding issues such as pricing, range of products, quality of product and the image of the business
- pay a large capital fee when buying the franchise and a percentage of profits thereafter

2.3 Copyrights, patents and trademarks

Entrepreneurs are keen to ensure that their efforts to generate new business ideas are protected from exploitation by rivals. A number of forms of protection exist:

- **Copyright.** This is the legal protection offered by the law to authors of written or recorded materials (e.g. books, films or music) for a specified period of time. Copyright gives authors and others the sole right to benefit from a work for up to 70 years and to sue any person who breaches that right.

- **Patents.** These provide the patent holder the sole right to make and sell the product they have invented for a period of up to 20 years.
- **Trademarks.** These normally take the form of distinctive symbols, words or logos, or a combination of them. They are indicated by the symbol ® and allow a business, a product or a brand to differentiate itself from competitors.

3 Transforming resources into goods and services

What you need to know:
- how businesses use inputs and, through a transformation process, convert them into goods and services
- the meaning of 'added value' in the context of different businesses

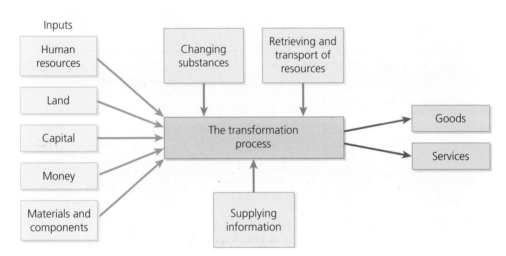

Figure 1.1 The transformation process

3.1 Inputs, outputs and the transformation process

Businesses use a range of inputs during production:
- **Human resources.** Businesses require a variety of human skills, both physical and mental. For example, a college might require the skills of lecturers, administrators and a maintenance team to keep the buildings and grounds in good condition. Businesses benefit from having conscientious employees with the right skills. Entrepreneurship is perhaps the most important human resource for a newly established business.
- **Land.** This is the site on which the business is based. It is important for all businesses, but especially agriculture and forestry (and other industries in the primary sector), where land needs to have particular characteristics such as the ability to grow specific crops or to yield up certain minerals.
- **Capital.** This refers to the man-made resources used by businesses. This is a large category of inputs encompassing machinery and vehicles, computers and furniture. Capital is required by all businesses and can improve the efficiency with which inputs are converted into outputs.
- **Money.** Cash is essential to finance day-to-day transactions and to ensure that bills can be paid on time. A newly established business often finds itself relatively short of this particular resource.

- **Materials and components.** This is another broad category. Manufacturers depend on supplies of raw materials and fuel, while service industries such as restaurants require food and drink to serve to customers.

The **transformation process** converts inputs into outputs. The process can take a variety of forms:

- **Changing the nature of substances.** BP and Shell convert the input of mineral oil by refining it into a form that it can be used as a fuel (petrol or diesel).
- **Supplying information that is available elsewhere.** This is what a travel agent does in the process of organising a holiday.
- **Retrieving resources and transporting them.** Mining companies extract resources from the ground and transport them to places where they are used.

Examiner's tip

It is important to think about inputs, outputs and the transformation process in relation to a variety of different businesses (those in the primary, secondary and tertiary sectors of the economy). This will help to prepare you for any particular scenario that you might encounter in the examination.

The outputs (generally termed 'products') of businesses can be broadly separated into two categories: goods and services. **Goods** have a physical existence and are the outputs of manufacturers. Examples of goods are cars, televisions, houses and bridges. In contrast, **services** are intangible — they do not exist physically. Gardeners, masseurs and financial advisers all provide services. Many businesses supply both goods and services. A health club might supply food (a good) as well as exercise classes (a service).

3.2 Adding value

Adding value is the process of increasing the worth or value of some resources by working on them. Thus, the value of a newly manufactured garden bench is greater than the raw materials that were put into it. The process of manufacturing has added value. Firms normally seek to maximise added value, either by minimising costs or by selling for the highest possible price. Some breweries add value to their products by creating theme pubs, enabling them to charge high prices for their products (beer, other drinks and meals), as consumers consider them to be of higher value.

Businesses commonly add value by creating a **unique selling point** or **proposition** (USP) for their products. A USP allows a business to differentiate its products from others in the market. This can help the business to develop advertising campaigns, assists in encouraging brand loyalty and may result in the firm charging a premium price. For example, Oil of Olay products claim to give users younger looking skin.

4 *Developing business plans*

What you need to know:
- the contents of a business plan
- the reasons for drawing up business plans
- the sources of information and guidance that may be used in drawing up a business plan

4.1 The contents of a business plan

A **business plan** is a document produced by a business when starting or expanding its operations, setting out its future activities, expenditure and income. The contents of a typical business plan are likely to include the following:

- **The type of business and the activity in which it is to be engaged.** The plan should establish the legal structure of the business (e.g. whether it is a company) and the product it is to supply.
- **The market in which the product is to be sold.** This section of the business plan should identify the target customers, the extent of the market and the business's competitors. This section should be based on market research.
- **The resources required.** Even the smallest businesses need some resources to be able to operate, such as property, machinery and raw materials. This part of the business plan will identify these as well as their expected costs.
- **The staff required for the business.** Although some small businesses do not employ people, many do. The business plan should set out the roles that will be carried out within the organisation.
- **Financial forecasts.** These are a vital element of all business plans. They are based on the sales forecast (and hence on market research) and set out the business's expected sales revenue and expenditure. This allows a forecast of profit (or loss) to be made. The business plan should also include a cash-flow forecast, setting out the expected inflows and outflows of cash each month.
- **Capital funding.** The plan should explain the amount of capital the business requires to purchase the resources (buildings, machinery, etc.) necessary to commence trading. It should also detail the proposed sources of funds and how much the entrepreneur is investing.
- **Details about the entrepreneur.** The plan should state the relevant experience and qualifications of the entrepreneur or entrepreneurs who are establishing the business.

Examiner's tip

The contents of a business plan are reflected in the range of material covered by Unit 1 of the specification. In studying this unit, you are looking at the concepts and topics that are included in a business plan.

4.2 Reasons for drawing up business plans

If an entrepreneur wishes to negotiate a loan to finance part of the start-up of a business, the potential investor will expect to see a detailed business plan. This helps the investor to assess the risk in lending money and also indicates that the entrepreneur has thought through his or her business plan fully.

The process of planning offers the entrepreneur an opportunity to assess the business idea in detail and to involve others in the process. At this stage, the entrepreneur may decide that it is not a good idea and abandon the plan.

However, if the entrepreneur does go ahead with the business, the plan can help in managing the business effectively. Plans set out goals or targets against which to make decisions. So, if sales are below expectations, the entrepreneur may decide to lower the price or spend more on advertising. They also allow the entrepreneur to judge whether the business is successful. For example, has it met its sales targets?

4.3 Sources of information and guidance for business planners

The information in business plans may come from several sources. Some sources may be expensive to use, but not as costly as making major errors in the planning process.

- **Other businesses.** An entrepreneur may talk to managers of other businesses who are not direct rivals. They may give information on costs of machinery and other equipment needed.
- **Professionals and advisers.** Estate agents may provide information on suitable property that is available and also expected costs, while solicitors may provide information on legal requirements and expenses. Banks will supply a range of expert advice. Many local authorities employ small business advisers to assist in the planning process.
- **Market research.** In some ways this is the most important source of information, especially if it is the result of primary market research. Potential customers can give invaluable information about whether a product meets the needs of the market and whether it is priced correctly, and can offer an insight into the possible level of sales. This last piece of information is vital in constructing financial forecasts in a business plan.

Conducting start-up market research

What you need to know:

- the methods of primary and secondary market research that are used by businesses
- how start-up businesses might use qualitative and quantitative market research
- the different approaches used in sampling

5.1 Primary and secondary market research

Market research is the process of gathering data on potential consumers. This research can provide information on the buying habits, lifestyle and perceptions of actual and potential consumers.

Market research entails one or more of the following:

- analysis of market potential for existing products
- forecasting likely demand for new products
- sales forecasting for all products
- study of market trends
- study of market characteristics
- analysis of market shares

One method of classifying market research is to separate it into primary and secondary research.

Primary research

Primary research collects primary data: that is, information that does not already exist. It is collected for a specific purpose by a market research agency or a business. It can be expensive and time consuming to collect, but should be accurate and precisely what the firm requires, possibly offering a competitive advantage.

Primary data are normally collected through **primary research** (also known as **field research**), which entails asking consumers questions directly. A number of techniques can be used to collect these data:

- **Surveys.** These can take a variety of forms. They may be based on a face-to-face interview and a questionnaire, possibly in the high street or in a retail outlet, or they may be conducted by telephone or post.
- **Observation.** This involves watching people in a variety of circumstances. It can provide information on how consumers might react to in-store displays, prices or the location of products.
- **Panels and group discussions.** Detailed questions are put to a small number of consumers. These are frequently used to discover consumers' attitudes to new products. They can also be used to collect information on changing consumer tastes and behaviour over time. The **Delphi technique** involves a panel of experts assembled to provide long-term forecasts, particularly on market trends, and relies on the panels in question reaching a consensus.
- **Test marketing.** This allows producers to try out a product on a small part of the market before a full-scale launch. Thus, an entrepreneur planning to start a business designing people's gardens might undertake a few commissions to test out his or her ideas before starting the job full time. Test marketing allows firms to iron out major faults in products before incurring the expense of a full launch. On the other hand, it gives competitors a preview of the new product and may permit an effective counter-strategy.

Secondary research

Secondary research (also termed **desk research**) collects **secondary data** — second-hand information gathered by someone else for another purpose at another time. Such data are relatively cheap to gather, but might be out of date or fail to answer the precise questions the firm wishes to pose.

A wide range of potential sources of such data are available to firms:

- **Official data.** The government and other agencies, such as the Department of Trade and Industry and the Central Statistical Office, produce vast amounts of detailed information. Key publications include the *Annual Abstract of Statistics* and business monitors.
- **Trade associations and trade journals.** These supply valuable and quite specific information on market trends.
- **Mintel and The Economist.** These produce reports on the markets for all types of products.
- **Internet.** The internet allows access to vast amounts of information about markets and consumer behaviour.

Examiner's tip

It is not enough to know the various methods of market research. You need to be able to make some assessment of their value in particular circumstances. It is worthwhile focusing on the cost of the various methods in comparison to the speed with which the data can be collected and their likely accuracy. Taking this sort of approach will encourage analytical writing.

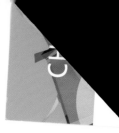

5.2 Qualitative and quantitative market research

Qualitative research

Qualitative market research is designed to discover the attitudes and opinions of consumers, which influence their purchasing behaviour. It is intended to uncover the reasons why consumers behave in particular ways. This allows businesses to design products that are more appealing to consumers and hopefully to achieve higher sales. Qualitative research is frequently based on the views of relatively small numbers of people through techniques such as consumer panels. It can be expensive to conduct this form of market research.

Quantitative research

Quantitative market research is the collection of information on consumer views and behaviour that can be analysed statistically. Whereas qualitative market research discovers 'why', this type of research reveals 'how many'. Thus, it is used to provide information on estimated sales, the size of the market and the prices that consumers are willing to pay. This type of market research can be conducted through primary market research (e.g. questionnaires and surveys) as well as through secondary market research.

5.3 Samples and sampling

It is most unlikely that a firm can collect information from all the consumers to whom it is hoping to sell. Such an approach would be too expensive and time consuming. Firms need to select a **sample** that is representative of the whole target market (known as the **population**). The general principle is that the larger the sample is, the more accurate the results are likely to be.

There are a number of ways in which samples can be collected:
- **Random sampling** means that each member of the population has an equal chance of being included. This is appropriate when a firm is researching a product aimed at a large target group. Because of the difficulties inherent in selecting a genuinely random sample, computers are often used to choose people.
- **Stratified random sampling** separates the population into segments or strata. This approach can avoid bias by ensuring that the composition of the sample accurately reflects that of the entire population.
- **Quota sampling** splits the population into a number of groups, each sharing common characteristics. For example, a survey might be conducted on the views of women regarding a new product, and the number of interviewees in each age category could be clearly set out. This saves money by limiting the number of respondents, although the quotas chosen may not accurately reflect the population who may purchase the product being researched.
- **Cluster sampling** involves selecting respondents from a small area chosen to reflect the market as a whole. The producer of a new real ale from a micro brewery, for example, may conduct intense research in one or two geographical locations.
- **Convenience sampling** is frequently used by people establishing a new business who have limited funds available. It entails sampling those consumers whom it can contact easily. Such research is susceptible to bias.

5.4 Factors influencing the choice of sampling methods

The most obvious factor affecting the choice of sampling method is the amount of finance available to the business. Obviously businesses with larger marketing budgets will spend more heavily and conduct research using larger samples. The nature of the product also has an impact, as the box below illustrates.

Ideas for application

The targets for a firm's market research campaign will depend heavily on the type of product, as will the methods used. For example, businesses researching business-to-business products, such as management consultancy, may conduct interviews with relatively small numbers of existing customers. In contrast, a business developing a consumer product, such as a new type of computer game, will be more likely to use questionnaires and surveys among larger numbers of people, most of whom should be potential customers.

Market research involves a fundamental trade-off between cost and accuracy. Firms require accurate information on which to base marketing decisions, such as:

- pricing policies
- product design
- types of promotion
- target customers at whom to aim the product

The greater the amount of information collected, the more reliable it should be, but the greater the cost to the firm. Many newly established businesses are on tight budgets, yet accurate market research is invaluable in aiding decision making. How much to spend on market research is a critical issue, and each set of circumstances requires a different decision. However, in each case, a business will compare expected costs and benefits.

Firms face a further dilemma. Even extensive (and expensive) market research cannot guarantee unbiased data. Respondents do not always tell the truth, samples do not always reflect the entire population accurately and the analysis of the raw data is not always correct.

6 *Understanding markets*

What you need to know:

- the types of market in which firms trade
- why demand is so important for start-up businesses
- how and why firms segment their markets
- the importance of, and how to calculate, market size, growth and share

6.1 The types of market in which firms trade

A **market** is a place or a means by which buyers and sellers come together to trade information and products. Some markets exist in specific locations, such as Smithfield meat market in London, while others are conducted mainly through telephone and computer-based communication, such as the market for company shares.

Markets can be classified into a range of different types:

- **Local markets.** These exist for goods and services for which it is not feasible to travel far, or for which products cannot be economically transported. Hairdressing and home delivery of take-away meals operate in local markets.
- **National markets.** These exist for products which sell throughout the UK. Some small breweries sell bottled beer to consumers throughout the country.
- **Physical markets.** These are markets that have specific locations. Many towns and villages have weekly markets that always take place at the same time and place. Some physical markets cater for people from a wider area, such as Hatton Garden in London which specialises in jewellery and especially diamonds.
- **Electronic markets.** The internet operates as a market for many small businesses, enabling them to reach a wider customer base than would otherwise be possible. eBay is an example of an electronic market.
- **Consumer markets.** These are very familiar markets in which sellers interact with the people who actually use their goods and services. They take place in high street shops and out-of-town shopping centres as well as electronically through mechanisms such as the internet.
- **Industrial markets.** In these markets, businesses sell products to other businesses. Hence they are also called **business-to-business markets**. An entrepreneur equipping a soon-to-be-opened restaurant may purchase kitchen equipment through dealing in industrial markets.

6.2 The importance of demand to start-up businesses

Demand is the quantity of a good or service that consumers wish to buy over a certain time period at a given price. A sufficient level of demand is absolutely essential for a new business. Without it, the business will not generate sufficient inflows of cash to pay bills as they become due, and in the longer term it will be unlikely to make a profit. One of the key points in a business plan is to look for evidence (probably in the form of the results of market research) that there will be sufficient demand for the new enterprise's products.

The environment in which a business trades is an important determinant of the level of demand for its products. There are a range of environmental factors that may influence the level of demand for a business's products:

- **The actions of competitors.** If the competition to a new business reacts to its arrival in the market by reducing prices, advertising more often or providing special offers such as free gifts, its will be more difficult for the new business to attract sufficient demand.
- **Consumers' incomes.** This is a particularly important factor influencing the level of demand for some products. A new business selling jewellery, foreign holidays or hot tubs might find that its sales depend on the level of incomes available for consumers to spend.
- **Seasonal factors.** Certain products sell particularly well at specific times of the year. A newly opened restaurant may attract more diners during holiday periods, while an ice-cream parlour will expect higher sales in the summer, especially if the weather is warm. Opening a new business at the 'wrong' time of year may result in low levels of demand.

However, decisions taken by the entrepreneur may also influence the level of demand for the business's products. Setting the right price for the product is important. If the price is too high, not enough consumers may purchase the product; if the price is too low, the business may not receive enough revenue to pay its costs. A price that represents good value and which takes into account those charged by close competitors is most likely to generate a good level of demand. The level of demand for the business's good or service also depends on the amount of advertising that the business engages in, and how successful that marketing is. Successful marketing makes customers aware of the product and helps to sell it to the target group of customers.

6.3 How and why firms segment their markets

Market segmentation involves dividing a market into identifiable sub-markets, each with its own customer characteristics. For example, brewers may sell certain beers to males aged 18–30. Market segments may be based on differences in:
- demographics — age, sex or social class
- psychographics — attitudes and tastes of consumers
- geography — for example, the various regions of the UK

Firms engage in market segmentation in order to:
- allow different marketing techniques/media to be employed
- increase the profit from each market segment
- assist in identifying new marketing opportunities
- use specialists in each of the market segments
- dominate certain segments
- reflect differences in customer tastes
- direct the marketing budget into those segments most likely to provide a higher return on the investment

Types of market segmentation

The following seven variables are known as **demographic factors** and form the basis of major types of market segmentation:
- **Age.** Some goods are aimed at young people, some at old. For example, music and fashion tend to be targeted at young consumers. Firms seek to target products at the appropriate groups. Someone starting a business offering gardening and DIY services may target older people who are less able to carry out such tasks themselves.
- **Sex.** Some products are specifically aimed at females, others at males. Businesses do not want to waste money trying to sell products to uninterested groupings. Magazines such as *Nuts* are promoted to reach young male audiences — during televised football matches, for example.
- **Family size and life cycle.** Family size is simply the number of family members. Family size determines the size of pack purchased and the type of product required.
- **Psychographic or lifestyle segmentation.** This seeks to classify people according to their values, opinions, personality characteristics and interests. It concentrates on the person rather than the product, and seeks to discover the unique lifestyles of consumers. Marketers aim to discover the number of people who might fall into each of these lifestyle categories, and then adapt products and services to suit the appropriate group.
- **Social class.** In reality, this type embraces social class and income. It is a method of segmentation that is crudely based on the occupation of the 'head of household'. It ignores second or subsequent wage earners. An example is the socioeconomic scale (Table 1.1), used by the UK market research industry to provide standardised social groupings. Similar classifications, such as the Hall Jones scale, are used elsewhere.

Social grade	Description of occupation	Example	% of population
A	Higher managerial and professional	Company director	3.0
B	Lower managerial and supervisory	Middle manager	20.4
C1	Non-manual	Bank clerk	27.2
C2	Skilled manual	Electrician	21.8
D	Semi-skilled and unskilled manual	Labourer	17.4
E	Those receiving no income from employment	Unemployed	10.2

Table 1.1 A socioeconomic scale

- **Neighbourhood classification.** This is a relatively new method of segmentation. ACORN (A Classification Of Residential Neighbourhoods) identifies 38 different types of residential neighbourhood according to demographic, housing and socioeconomic characteristics. The classification breaks the whole country down into units of 150 dwellings, with the predominant type being the classification adopted for that unit. Major users of the system include direct-mail companies, financial institutions, gas and electricity companies, charities, political parties and credit-card companies. ACORN was developed by CACI information services and has been widely used in siting stores and posters.
- **Education.** This is a less useful factor on which to base segmentation because it assumes that there is a strong correlation between educational attainment, income levels and expenditure patterns. Firms target luxury products at those whom they determine to be higher income earners. Newspaper readership is often used as a proxy for education, the assumption being that more highly educated people read newspapers such as the *Independent* and *The Times*.

Two other, more specialised, variables also exist:
- **Benefit segmentation.** This groups people on the basis of why they have bought a product. Different people buy the same product for a variety of reasons. People might buy a satellite dish, for example, to watch sport, because of a special offer, to be the first in the street to have satellite or because they are bored with terrestrial television. This approach may identify an unsatisfied market segment that the business can target.
- **Usage segmentation.** This recognises that consumption rates of goods and services are not evenly distributed within the population. If a company can identify the heaviest users, it can target them in its marketing. If, for example, the small brewery wanted to advertise beer on local radio, it would be likely to choose slots in programmes that would listened to by men.

6.4 Market size, growth and share

Market size

Market size is the total demand for a particular product. This can be measured in two ways:
- **By volume.** This is the number of products sold.
- **By value.** This is the amount of spending on the product and is calculated by multiplying the average price of the product by the number of units sold. For example, the number (or volume) of two-person tents sold in England in one year might be 215,000. If they sell at an average price of £90, the size of this market in value terms will be 215,000 × £90 = £19,350,000 or £19.35 million.

Market growth

Market growth takes place when the size of a market increases. This is normally measured in percentage terms. So, if the market for two-person tents in England increases to £21 million, it will have grown in size. The rate at which the market has grown can be measured using the following formula:

$$\text{market growth rate} = \frac{\text{change in market size}}{\text{original market size}} \times 100$$

$$= \frac{£1.65 \text{ million}}{£19.35 \text{ million}} \times 100 = 8.53\%$$

Of course, markets do not always grow. If sales in this market changed from £19.35 million to £18 million, then it would have become smaller. This would result in a negative growth rate. In this example it would be −£1.35 million/£19.35 million × 100 = −6.98%.

Market share

Market share is the percentage of total sales in a market which is achieved by one specific firm. If a particular business has annual sales of two-person tents in England worth £1.935 million and the market size is £19.35 million, its market share could be calculated as shown below.

$$\text{market share} = \frac{\text{the business's sales}}{\text{total market sale}} \times 100$$

$$= \frac{£1.935 \text{ million}}{£19.35 \text{ million}} \times 100 = 10\%$$

If the market increases in size over a year and the business's sales rise more slowly over the same time, or even fall, then the business's market share will fall. In contrast, if the business's sales increase more rapidly than the market growth rate, its market share will rise. Finally, in the unlikely event of the firm's sales rising at the same rate as the market grows, its market share will be unchanged.

Market share is an important measure of a firm's success in a market. Rising market share is desirable for many businesses and some state it as a target.

Examiner's tip

It is important that you understand and are able to calculate market size, growth and share. Most of these calculations are based on percentages. Do practise these calculations using a variety of different figures.

7 Choosing the right legal structure for a business

What you need to know:
- the benefits and drawbacks of sole traders, partnerships, private limited companies and public limited companies
- the nature of not-for-profit businesses and the objectives they pursue

7.1 Sole traders, partnerships, private limited companies and public limited companies

The different kinds of business fall into two broad categories of business: corporate and non-corporate, as shown in Table 1.2.

Non-corporate businesses	Corporate businesses
Sole traders (or proprietors)	Private limited companies
Partnerships	Public limited companies

Table 1.2 Types of business

Corporate businesses

Corporate businesses have a legal identity that is separate from that of their owners — this is termed **limited liability**. It means that a company can sue and be sued and can enter into contracts. Limited liability has an important implication for the owners (share-holders) of corporate businesses because, in the event of such a business failing, the shareholders' private possessions are safe. Their liability is limited to the amount they have invested.

There are two methods by which the liability of shareholders can be limited:
- **By shares.** In this case a shareholder's liability is limited to the value of the shares that he or she has purchased. There can be no further call on the shareholder's wealth.
- **By guarantee.** Each member's liability is restricted to the amount he or she has agreed to pay in the event of the business being wound up. This is more common with not-for-profit businesses, which we consider below.

There are two main types of corporate company:
- **Private limited companies.** These are normally much smaller than public limited companies. Share capital must not exceed £50,000 and 'Ltd' must be included after the company's name. The shares of a private limited company cannot be bought and sold without the agreement of other shareholders. This, and the fact that the company cannot be listed on the Stock Exchange, means that private limited companies are likely to remain small.
- **Public limited companies.** The shares of these companies can be sold on the Stock Exchange and purchased by any business or individual. Public limited companies must be registered as public companies and have the term 'plc' after their name. They must have a minimum capital of £50,000 by law; in practice, this figure is likely to be far higher. Public limited companies have to publish more details of their financial affairs than private limited companies.

Non-corporate businesses

Non-corporate businesses and their owners are not treated as separate entities — all an owner's private possessions can be sold to settle the business's debts in the event of bankruptcy. Sole traders and partners are usually said to have **unlimited liability**.

The different types of non-corporate business are as follows:
- **Sole traders (or proprietors).** These are businesses owned by a single person, although the business may have a number of employees. Such one-person businesses are common in retailing and services such as plumbing and hairdressing.
- **Partnerships.** These comprise between 2 and 20 people who contribute capital and expertise to a business. The Partnership Act of 1890 established the legal rules under which partnerships operate. A partnership is usually based on a Deed of Partnership, which sets out how much capital each partner has contributed, the share of profits each partner shall receive and the rules for electing new partners. Some partners may be 'sleeping partners', contributing capital but taking no active part in the operation of the business. Partnerships are common in the professions: for example, solicitors, dentists and accountants.

Those forming a company must send two main documents to the Registrar of Companies:
- **Memorandum of Association.** This sets out details of the company's name and address and its objectives in trading.
- **Articles of Association.** This details the internal arrangements of the company, including frequency of shareholders' meetings and distribution of profits.

Once these documents have been approved, the company receives a Certificate of Incorporation and can commence trading.

The advantages and disadvantages of the various legal forms of business are shown in Table 1.3.

7.2 Not-for profit businesses

Not all businesses aim to make profits. A not-for–profit business is any organisation that has business objectives other than making a profit. These businesses are also called **social enterprises**.

Social enterprises trade in a wide range of industries and operate with a number of non-profit objectives:
- **To provide services to local communities.** Some social enterprises may remove graffiti or clean up beaches to the benefit of entire communities.
- **To give people job-related skills.** The TV chef, Jamie Oliver, runs a chain of restaurants (called 'Fifteen') with the prime objective of providing training in a variety of catering skills for young people from disadvantaged backgrounds.
- **Fair trading activities.** Some businesses import products from poor societies overseas but pay above the market price for the products, and often also invest in facilities such as education and healthcare for the exporting communities. Cafédirect imports coffee under fair trade principles.

Type of business	Advantages	Disadvantages
Sole trader	• Simple and cheap to establish with few legal formalities. • The owner receives all the profits (if there are any). • Able to respond quickly to changes in the market. • Confidentiality is maintained as financial details do not have to be published.	• The owner is likely to be short of capital for investment and expansion. • Few assets for collateral to support applications for loans. • Unlimited liability. • It can be difficult for sole traders to take holidays.
Partnership	• Between them partners may have a wide range of skills and knowledge. • Partners are able to raise greater amounts of capital than sole traders. • The pressure on owners is reduced as cover is available for holidays and there is support in making decisions.	• Control is shared between the partners. • Arguments are common among partners. • There is still an absolute shortage of capital — even 20 people can only raise so much. • Unlimited liability.
Private limited company	• Shareholders benefit from limited liability. • Companies have access to greater amounts of capital. • Private companies are only required to divulge a limited amount of financial information. • Companies have a separate legal identity.	• Private limited companies cannot sell their shares on the Stock Exchange. • Requiring permission to sell shares limits potential for flexibility and growth. • Limited companies have to conform to a number of expensive administrative formalities.
Public limited company	• Public companies can gain positive publicity as a result of trading on the Stock Exchange. • Stock exchange quotation offers access to large amounts of capital. • Stock Exchange rules are strict and this encourages investors to part with their money. • Suppliers will be more willing to offer credit to public companies.	• A Stock Exchange listing means emphasis is placed on short-term financial results not long-term performance. • Public companies are required to publish a great deal of financial information. • Trading as a public limited company can result in hefty administrative expenses.

Table 1.3 The advantages and disadvantages of different legal forms of business

8   *Raising finance*

What you need to know:

- the sources of finance for start-up businesses
- the advantages and disadvantages of the various sources of finance
- the circumstances in which particular types of finance might be most appropriate

8.1 The sources of finance for start-up businesses

A start-up business needs capital to purchase the assets required to start trading. The types of asset will depend upon the type of business. Retailers may need to purchase stock for their shop and possibly a property, while a garden centre would need land and greenhouses to grow plants. Start-up capital may also be used to pay for marketing the business (e.g. advertising), and for hiring and training staff.

Personal sources of finance

Many small businesses are started using the entrepreneur's own money. Some entrepreneurs might have been made redundant and have received a relatively large sum of money in compensation. Others may use savings or a lump sum of capital paid as part of a pension to raise the necessary finance. Finally, many entrepreneurs ask friends and family to provide money for their start-up capital.

Loan capital

Loan capital is finance that is used by a business which has been borrowed from external sources, such as a bank. There are different types of loan capital:

- **Bank overdraft.** Cheap and easy to obtain, a bank overdraft is repayable on demand. This allows a business to meet its short-term commitments and it only pays interest on the amount and for the period that it is in overdraft.
- **Short-term loans.** These are loans given for specific purposes rather than for use as working capital. Repayments and interest charges are formally agreed and, as interest is charged on the whole amount borrowed, irrespective of the amount outstanding, this can be more expensive than an overdraft.
- **Medium-term loans.** These are usually obtained from high-street banks but can also be raised from specialist investment companies that concentrate on providing medium-term finance. These loans can be repaid in instalments over the loan period or by a one-off sum at an agreed date. The interest rate charged can be fixed or variable, which is usually determined by negotiation.
- **Long-term loans.** These are used to purchase capital assets such as buildings or other businesses that have a long life. Long-term loans usually have a fixed rate of interest and are given only after an independent survey of the asset. In addition, a comprehensive report on the business's past and future expected performance is compiled. A mortgage loan is one that is usually secured on land or buildings for periods of 20 years or longer.

Share capital

Share capital is finance invested into a company as a result of the purchase of shares, thereby providing the company with sums of capital. In return, shareholders are granted part-ownership of the company. They have the right to a say in certain company decisions and may receive a share of the company's profits (in the form of dividends), assuming that any are earned.

Ideas for application

It is important to consider the type of business when answering questions on sources of finance. It may seem obvious, but relatively few students suggest that newly formed companies can raise funds by selling shares.

Venture capital

Venture capital is finance advanced to businesses judged to be relatively high risk, in the form of share capital and loan capital. Financial institutions (e.g. merchant banks) often provide venture capital to start-up businesses, as do a small number of wealthy individuals, known as **business angels**.

Entrepreneurs might need to sell some shares (usually a minority holding) in their companies to venture capitalists to persuade them to invest in the business. The investment by venture capitalists in start-up businesses normally takes the form of loan and share capital.

Venture capitalists not only provide finance but also offer experience, contacts and advice when necessary to new entrepreneurs.

8.2 The advantages and disadvantages of the various sources of finance

Each of the sources of finance we have identified has advantages and disadvantages for entrepreneurs, as shown in Table 1.4.

8.3 The circumstances in which particular types of finance might be most appropriate

Certain sources of finance are most appropriate in particular situations. Personal sources are likely to be used as part of the start-up capital for many new businesses. However,

Source of capital	Advantages	Disadvantages
Personal sources	• Normally allows the entrepreneur to retain complete control of the business. • May be a relatively cheap source of finance and can be interest-free.	• Is unlikely to provide large sums of finance. • Friends and family may ask for repayment of loans at short notice.
Loan capital	• Loan capital can be arranged at relatively short notice. • Some forms of loans (e.g. overdrafts) are very flexible and can be tailored to the business's needs.	• Businesses are committed to interest payments at a time when they may have relatively small earnings. • An unexpected rise in interest rates can increase a start-up business's costs.
Share capital	• This can be a relatively flexible source of finance as dividends will only be paid to shareholders if a large enough profit is made. • The entrepreneur has to share profits with other owners of the business.	• If an entrepreneur sells too many shares in the company, he or she may lose control of the business. • In most circumstances, private limited companies cannot sell additional shares without the approval of all shareholders.
Venture capital	• This is a good means of raising finance for risky start-up businesses. • Venture capitalists may offer advice and guidance to new entrepreneurs in managing the business.	• A venture capitalist may want a large share of any profits in return for making an investment. • The entrepreneur and the venture capitalist may disagree over the future direction of the new business.

Table 1.4 Sources of capital: advantages and disadvantages

they may play a more significant role if the business requires relatively small amounts of capital (e.g. a website design business) or if the entrepreneur is wealthy.

Loans may be easier to organise and available at lower rates of interest if the business has assets, such as property that can be used as security against the loan. This is known as **collateral** and would be sold by the creditor (often a bank) to repay the entire loan if the new enterprise defaulted on its repayments. People with successful experience as entrepreneurs may find it easier to negotiate loans.

The most obvious point about share capital is that companies alone can raise capital in this way — it is not possible for sole traders or partnerships to sell shares. This is often used to raise only a part of the start-up capital required.

Venture capital is most appropriate for high-risk enterprises. A high-risk enterprise is one that has a higher than normal chance of failing. These might be enterprises that are unique, or which involve entrepreneurs with little or no experience of running a business.

9 Locating the business

What you need to know:
- the factors that influence a start-up business's location decision
- how the relative importance of these factors varies according to circumstances

9.1 The factors that influence start-up location decisions

Most businesses seek locations that will help them to make profits and, for many new businesses, to survive the tricky first few months of trading when they are particularly vulnerable. Entrepreneurs will consider one or more of the factors below when deciding on a location for a new business:

- **The market.** A business needs to be located near to its customers to make it as easy as possible for them to use its services or to buy its products. For example, a fast-food restaurant will want to be located where there are large numbers of people passing by.
- **Competition.** It is common for estate agents to locate close to one another, as when consumers are looking to purchase houses, they are likely to visit all local agents — as long as it is convenient to do so. An estate agent that locates some distance away might miss out on many potential customers.
- **Infrastructure.** Some businesses require good transport links to operate effectively. Thus, a business that relies on the delivery of bulky or heavy products may want to be close to high-quality rail and road links.
- **Technology.** Many entrepreneurs seek to work from home. Accountants, writers and artists are examples of occupations in which this is possible. A high-speed internet connection (broadband) is often a crucial element in a decision to work from home. The widespread availability of broadband in the UK has freed many businesses in terms of location.
- **Climate and natural resources.** This is very important for some industries, such as tourism and agriculture. A seaside hotel targeting families will want to be located near to a safe and sandy beach.
- **Suppliers.** Some businesses rely heavily upon particular suppliers and the need to be close to them may be the most important locational factor. A business that smokes fish is highly likely to locate close to a fishing port.

● **Qualitative factors.** Most of the above locational factors assist a business to maximise its revenue from sales or to minimise the costs it has to pay. However, some entrepreneurs consider qualitative factors. They might wish to live in a specific location to be near friends or family, or because they enjoy the countryside or climate.

9.2 How the relative importance of these factors varies according to circumstances

It is important to consider how the relative importance of these factors might vary according to the type of business. Retail businesses are strongly influenced by the market and by a factor known as 'footfall': that is, they want to be in a location where there are plenty of customers passing by and possibly an area that is known for that type of business. The market is also important for other service businesses, especially those that supply personal services. It is common to find hairdressers and beauty therapists in relatively highly populated areas, so that they are near to potential customers.

Businesses in the primary sector might be heavily influenced by natural factors. A fruit farm will want suitable land and an appropriate climate. Similarly, a tree surgeon is likely to have a flourishing business in a wooded area.

Manufacturers may depend heavily on suppliers and therefore seek to locate close to them. This might be especially true if the supplies are heavy or bulky, and therefore expensive to transport. A cider maker is likely to site its business near to apple orchards. It is probably cheaper to transport the finished cider to the market than to transport large quantities of apples over long distances.

Examiner's tip

The above are just general rules that are intended to help you to think about the precise needs of an individual business when deciding on a location. Each location decision is different and needs to be judged separately.

---

10 *Employing people*

What you need to know:
● the types of employee used in small businesses
● the ways in which start-up businesses can use consultants and advisers
● the reasons for and drawbacks of employing people in a start-up business

10.1 The types of employee used in small businesses

New businesses may not have any employees — the only person working in the business might be the entrepreneur. However, it is not unusual for even the newest business to hire employees, and these employees can be divided into a number of categories:
● **Full-time employees.** Full-time employees work in the business for a whole working week each week. The number of hours that is considered to be full time will vary according to the type of business, but is commonly between 35 and 40.

- **Part-time employees.** This category of employee works less than full-time hours. This may be 2 or 3 days each week or it could be shorter hours each day (say, 10 a.m. until 3 p.m.) because of childcare responsibilities.
- **Permanent employees.** Permanent employees remain with a business until they decide to leave or their employment is ended for one of a limited number of reasons allowed by the law.
- **Temporary employees.** This category of employee is only employed for a set period of time. This is agreed at the time the employment commences. Temporary employment is commonly arranged to cover period in which the business is particularly busy or to cover for other permanent employees who are absent from work for reasons such as maternity leave.

10.2 The ways in which start-up businesses can use consultants and advisers

Consultants and advisers have specialist skills that can be of great value to entrepreneurs, especially during the start-up stage of the business. They can offer a range of support to businesses, including the following aspects of a business's operations:
- constructing and conducting a programme of market research
- devising an effective marketing strategy
- recruiting the best available employees
- overcoming operational issues, such as providing high-quality service
- preparing business plans in support of loan applications

Consultants and advisers are hired to complete a specific task or tasks. They are often highly experienced managers or entrepreneurs, who can bring great experience to the solution of a range of business issues and problems. Hiring consultants and advisers can be expensive, but their support can be of enormous value to entrepreneurs and may help to ensure the survival of a fledgling enterprise. They may be paid a daily rate while working for the start-up business or a flat fee for completing the task.

Examiner's tip

A benefit from the use of consultants and advisers can come before the business starts trading, when they can help to decide whether a proposed enterprise is viable.

10.3 The reasons for and drawbacks of employing people in a start-up business

Employing people in their business offers significant benefits to entrepreneurs. It is unlikely that an entrepreneur will have the full range of skills necessary to manage a business successfully. Some entrepreneurs have excellent selling and marketing skills, but know little about managing finance; others might have great abilities in the areas of production and design, but limited understanding of managing and leading people. Entrepreneurs can employ people to support them and to provide the skills and knowledge they do not possess.

10 Employing people

The workload of an entrepreneur can be immense. Working very long hours may not result in an entrepreneur being able to give an optimal performance. Employing people to carry out routine duties in the business can allow for time off and also for precious holidays.

However, hiring people does bring problems and complications. Entrepreneurs have to conform with UK and EU employment law if they decide to employ people. This law is comprehensive and covers issues such as advertising vacancies, recruiting staff, paying employees and providing safe and healthy working environments. Employees may not carry out their duties to the standard expected, or they may fall ill, requiring prolonged periods off work. Employees may become parents and therefore be entitled to periods off work during which they have to be paid.

Employing people can bring great benefits to start-up businesses, but only if the right employees are hired.

CHAPTER 2 Financial planning

1 Calculating costs, revenues and profits

What you need to know:

- the distinctions between fixed, variable and total costs, and how they are calculated
- the relationship between price and total revenue
- the importance of profit and how it is calculated

1.1 Fixed, variable and total costs, and how they are calculated

Fixed costs

Fixed costs are expenses that do not vary in line with changes in demand or output: that is, they remain constant over the time period being considered. They have to be paid whether any products are made and sold or not. Examples of fixed costs are:

- rent
- depreciation
- salaries
- interest charges

Variable costs

Variable costs are those costs incurred by a business that vary in direct relation to the level of output and demand: that is, as output rises or falls, so do variable costs. Examples of variable costs include:

- materials
- power
- components
- shop-floor labour costs

Many entrepreneurs calculate the variable cost of producing a single unit of output (for example, a bottle of wine or a single hotel guest). This figure (which is termed **variable cost per unit**) can then be multiplied by the number of units of output to give **total variable costs**. Variable cost per unit is also useful in calculating breakeven point, as we shall see in section 2.

Total costs

Total costs can be calculated by using this formula:

total costs = fixed costs + variable costs

Entrepreneurs should know the total costs of the business, as this can help with pricing decisions. If an entrepreneur can set his or her prices at a level that covers the business's total costs, then it will make a profit. However, this assumes that the products will sell at the chosen price and that sufficient numbers will be sold.

Figure 2.1 shows how fixed, variable and total costs alter as output increases, as well as the relationship between the three types of cost.

As total costs are the sum of fixed and variable costs, the lines representing variable and total costs are parallel in Figure 2.1. This is because the difference between them is fixed costs, which do not change when output changes.

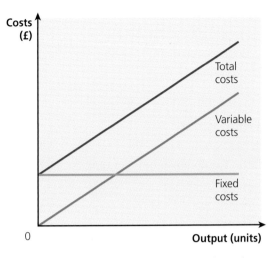

Figure 2.1 A graph showing fixed costs, variable costs and total costs

1.2 The relationship between price and total revenue

Revenue is the total value of sales made by a business over a specified period of time. This is also called **sales revenue** or **total revenue**. Revenue is calculated by using the formula:

revenue = quantity sold × selling price per unit

However, there is a complex relationship between price and revenue. An increase in price does not automatically increase a business's revenue. Whether revenue increases or not following a price rise depends on how many customers stop buying the product. If a price rise leads to many customers deciding to stop buying the product, it may result in a fall in revenue. On the other hand, if most customers continue to buy the product, sales revenue will increase following a price rise.

A start-up business will benefit from market research into how sensitive the demand of potential customers is to changes in the price of the product.

1.3 The importance of profit and how it is calculated

Profit is the amount that is left over from revenue after all costs incurred in earning that revenue have been deducted. It is given by:

profit = sales revenue — total cost

Calculating profit may require you to use the following formula:

profit = revenue – (fixed costs + variable costs)

The box overleaf shows some examples of how to calculate profit.

Examples

Imagine a firm has a selling price of £10 per unit, variable cost per unit of £5 and fixed costs of £60,000.

(1) Profit or loss at output and sales of 5,000 units:

		£
Sales revenue (£10 × 5,000 units)		50,000
Variable costs (£5 × 5,000 units)	25,000	
Fixed costs	60,000	
Total costs		85,000
Loss		(35,000)

(2) Profit or loss at output and sales of 15,000 units:

		£
Sales revenue (£10 × 15,000 units)		150,000
Variable costs (£5 × 15,000 units)	75,000	
Fixed costs	60,000	
Total costs		135,000
Profit		15,000

Note how revenue and variable costs change when the level of output and sales is altered.

Knowing how to calculate the various component parts of a firm's costs, revenues and profit is, of course, important. However, it is the relationship between these parts that really allows analysis, planning and decision making to take place.

Profit is important for most entrepreneurs when starting a business. It is the reward for taking a risk in starting a business and also for those people who may have invested in it. It may be that a new business does not make a profit during the early stages of trading. It can take time to build up a sufficient customer base to generate enough revenue to cover the total costs of production.

Examiner's tip

Remember that some businesses do not aim to make a profit. These businesses are called not-for-profit businesses or social enterprises.

2   Using breakeven analysis to make decisions

What you need to know:
- the meaning of contribution and how to calculate it and contribution per unit
- the meaning of breakeven and how to calculate it
- how to construct a breakeven chart
- how to analyse the effect of changes on breakeven charts
- the strengths and weaknesses of breakeven analysis

2.1 Contribution and contribution per unit

Contribution

Contribution is the difference between sales revenue and variable cost. It is calculated using the following formula:

contribution = sales revenue — variable costs

Contribution is a simple concept, yet one which is very important to all businesses, particularly to those that produce a number of products. It is used in the first place to pay a company's fixed costs, which are notionally paid first. Once these have been covered, any additional contributions are used to provide profits for the company.

Example

A start-up business may plan to produce two products: A and B.

	Product A	Product B
Price per unit	£10	£25
Variable cost per unit	£6	£15
Forecast sales (units)	10,000	35,000
Total contribution	£40,000	£350,000

In each case, we have simply deducted the variable cost of per unit production from the selling price per unit of the product before multiplying by sales to arrive at total contribution.

Contribution per unit

The idea of contribution is that each individual product has to make a contribution to the overall running costs of the firm. As long as the selling price of an individual product is greater than the variable costs associated with making the product, the product will make a contribution to paying the overheads of the business and eventually generate profit.

Contribution per unit can be calculated in two ways:

(1) unit selling price – unit variable costs = contribution per unit

(2) $\dfrac{\text{total sales revenue – total variable cost}}{\text{output}}$ = contribution per unit

2.2 The meaning of breakeven and how to calculate it

Breakeven occurs at the level of output at which a business's total costs exactly equal its revenue or earnings, and neither a profit nor a loss is incurred.

At breakeven point, the business has made insufficient sales to make a profit, but sufficient sales to avoid a loss. In other words, it has earned just enough to cover its costs. This occurs when total cost = sales total revenue.

Breakeven analysis can provide businesses with important information. The most important element of this information is an indication of how much the firm needs to produce (and sell) in order to make a profit.

The breakeven point can be calculated using this formula:

$$\text{breakeven in units of output} = \frac{\text{fixed costs}}{\text{selling price} - \text{variable cost per unit}}$$

Example

Look again at the example of calculating profits and losses on page 28. The firm in question sold its products for £10 each, incurred a variable cost on each unit of £5 and had fixed costs of £60,000. Using the formula above:

$$\text{breakeven} = \frac{60{,}000}{(£10 - £5)} = \frac{60{,}000}{5} = 12{,}000 \text{ units}$$

Thus, if the firm produces and sells 12,000 units, its costs will exactly equal its revenues and it will break even.

Contribution and breakeven

The theory of contribution tells us that if each product makes a contribution, and all these contributions are added up and used to pay fixed costs, any contributions remaining at this point are profit.

This enables us to use the theory of contribution to calculate breakeven and profit for any given situation. The question is: how many individual contributions are needed to pay fixed costs? This is given by:

$$\frac{\text{fixed costs}}{\text{contribution per unit}} = \frac{\text{number of}}{\text{contributions needed}} = \frac{\text{level of output}}{\text{to break even}}$$

At this point, enough contributions have been made to pay fixed costs. Variable costs have already been accounted for because contribution = sales revenue − variable cost.

This is a very useful formula, as it enables businesses to model 'what if' scenarios quickly and easily without having to redraw breakeven charts all the time.

2.3 How to construct a breakeven chart

The easiest way of representing the breakeven point is through the use of a breakeven chart or diagram, as shown in Figure 2.2. The step-by-step points below explain how to draw a breakeven chart:

(1) Give the chart a title.

(2) Label axes (horizontal — output in units; vertical — costs/revenues in pounds).

(3) Draw on the fixed cost line.

(4) Draw on the variable cost line.

(5) Draw on the total cost line.

(6) Draw on the sales revenue line.

(7) Label the breakeven point where sales revenue = total cost.

(8) Mark on the selected operating point (SOP): that is, the actual or forecast level of the company's output.

(9) Mark on the margin of safety (the difference between the SOP and the breakeven level of output).

(10) Mark clearly the amount of profit and loss. Note that this is a vertical distance at any given level of production, and not an area.

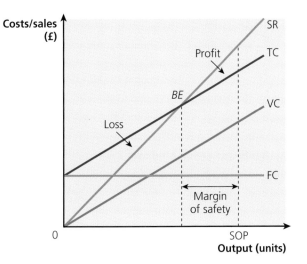

Figure 2.2 A breakeven chart for product X

Examiner's tip

Because of time constraints, in an examination it is unlikely that you will be asked to draw a complete breakeven chart from scratch. It is more probable that you will be asked to add lines to an incomplete chart or to alter the position of existing lines following changes in costs or prices. You should practise these types of activity.

2.4 How to analyse the effect of changes on breakeven charts

Breakeven analysis can illustrate the effects of changes in price and costs, and assist entrepreneurs in making decisions, such as through a number of 'what if?' scenarios:
- What level of output and sales will be needed to break even if we sell at a price of £x per unit?
- What would be the effect on the level of output and sales needed to break even of an x% rise (or fall) in fixed or variable costs?

Using breakeven analysis in these circumstances, entrepreneurs can decide whether it is likely to be profitable to supply a product at a certain price or to start production. This aspect of breakeven analysis makes it a valuable technique. After all, few businesses trade in environments in which changes in prices and costs do not occur regularly.

Figure 2.3 illustrates the effects of changes in key variables on the breakeven chart. These are further illustrated in Table 2.1.

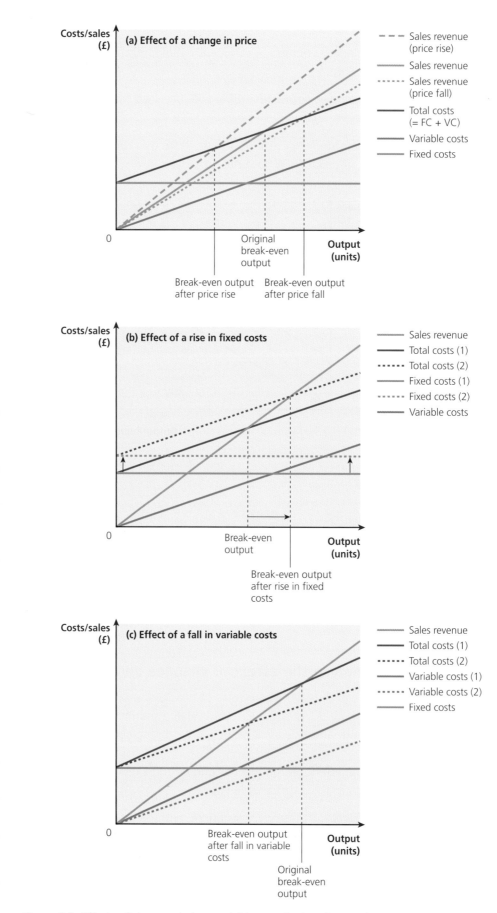

Figure 2.3 Effects of changes in key variables on the breakeven chart

Note: Figure 2.3(b) only illustrates a rise in fixed costs to avoid the diagram becoming too complex. A fall in fixed costs would have the exact opposite effect. For the same reason, Figure 2.3(c) only illustrates a fall in variable costs. A rise in variable costs would have the exact opposite effect.

Change in key variable	Impact on breakeven chart	Effect on breakeven output	Explanation of change	Illustrated in figure
Increase in selling price	Revenue line pivots upwards.	Breakeven is reached at a lower level of output.	Fewer sales will be necessary to break even because each sale generates more revenue, while costs have not altered.	Figure 2.3(a)
Fall in selling price	Revenue line pivots downwards.	A higher level of output is necessary to reach break even.	Each sale will earn less revenue for the business and, because costs have not altered, more sales will be required to breakeven.	Figure 2.3(a)
Rise in fixed costs	Parallel upward shift in fixed and total cost lines.	Breakeven occurs at a higher level of output.	More sales will be required to break even because the business has to pay higher costs before even starting production.	Figure 2.3(b)
Fall in fixed costs	Parallel downward shift in fixed and total cost lines.	Smaller output required to break even.	Because the business faces lower costs, less sales will be needed to ensure that revenue matches costs.	
Rise in variable costs	Total cost line pivots upwards.	Higher output needed to break even.	Each unit of output costs more to produce, so a greater number of sales will be necessary if the firm is to break even.	
Fall in variable costs	Total cost line pivots downwards.	Lower level of output needed to break even.	Every unit of production is produced more cheaply, so less output and sales are necessary to break even.	Figure 2.3(c)

Table 2.1 Effects of changes in key variables on the breakeven chart

2.5 The strengths and weaknesses of breakeven analysis

Strengths of breakeven

Breakeven analysis has the following strengths:

- **Starting a new business.** An entrepreneur can estimate the level of sales required before the business would start to make a profit. From this, the entrepreneur can see whether or not the business proposal is viable. The results of market research are important here.
- **Supporting loan applications.** Entrepreneurs will be unlikely to succeed in negotiating a loan with a bank unless they have carried out a range of financial planning, including breakeven analysis.
- **Measuring profit and losses.** In diagrammatic form, breakeven enables businesses to tell at a glance what their estimated level of profit or loss would be at any level of output and sales.

- **Modelling 'what if?' scenarios.** Breakeven enables businesses to model what will happen to their level of profit if they change prices or are faced by changes in costs.

Examiner's tip

It is common for examination questions to ask you to read off data from breakeven charts. You may be required to read off profit or loss, revenue or variable costs. You should practise doing this.

Limitations of breakeven

Breakeven analysis is quick to perform but it is a simplification. As such, it has several shortcomings:

- No costs are truly fixed. A stepped fixed cost line would be a better representation, as fixed costs are likely to increase in the long term and at higher levels of output if more production capacity is required.
- A linear (straight) variable cost line takes no account of the discounts available for bulk buying.
- The total cost line should not, therefore, be represented by a straight line.
- Sales revenue assumes that all output produced is sold and at a uniform price, which is unrealistic.
- The analysis is only as good as the information provided. Collecting accurate information is expensive, and in many cases the cost of collection would outweigh any benefit that breakeven analysis could provide.

3 *Using cash-flow forecasting*

What you need to know:
- the nature of cash flow
- how to forecast cash flow
- the structure of a cash-flow forecast
- why businesses forecast cash flow

3.1 The nature of cash flow

Cash flow is the amount of money moving into and out of a business over a period of time. Cash flow is important for businesses, especially newly established businesses, because it indicates their ability to pay bills as they become due. Most new businesses will encounter periods when outflows of funds are larger than inflows. It is vital that entrepreneurs are aware of such periods and make plans to manage them.

Examiner's tip

Please avoid saying that the difference between cash inflows and outflows is profit. Cash flow relates to timing — a profitable business may run short of cash if customers do not pay on time. Many new businesses also have to spend large sums of money on advertising, materials and paying wages (creating cash outflows) some time before they receive any cash inflows. It may be that the business is very profitable once it receives payment — if it survives that long.

3.2 How to forecast cash flow

Cash-flow forecasts are constructed using a number of potential sources. The starting point is to use market research to establish the likely demand for the new good or service. This is more likely to be accurate if primary research is conducted, although this is a relatively expensive option at a time when a business is likely to face heavy costs in other areas. Secondary market research may also provide useful information on future inflows of cash, and may be especially helpful concerning issues such as seasonal fluctuations in sales.

Outflows of cash can be more easily estimated once the entrepreneur knows the expected levels of sales. The entrepreneur then has some idea of the amount of fuel, labour, materials and other resources that will be required. The entrepreneur can therefore estimate outflows that are likely to take place.

It can often be difficult to forecast cash flows accurately for new businesses. It may not be feasible to conduct sufficient primary research due to cost or time constraints. The reactions of competitors to the arrival of the new business in the market may not have been allowed for. They might respond by cutting prices or implementing promotional campaigns, and therefore inflows of cash for the new business may be lower than expected.

3.3 The structure of a cash-flow forecast

Cash-flow forecasts are a central part of a business plan for a new business. They comprise three sections:
- **Receipts** — recording the expected total month-by-month receipts.
- **Payments** — recording the expected monthly expenditure by item.
- **Running balance** — keeping a running total of the expected bank balance at the beginning and end of each month (see Figure 2.4). These are termed **opening and closing balances**. The closing balance at the end of one month becomes the opening balance at the start of the next month.

Negative figures in cash-flow forecasts are usually shown in brackets.

Month	Jan	Feb	Mar	Apr	May	June
Receipts						
1 Sales cash	4,500					
2 Sales credit	3,650					
3 Total cash in (1 + 2)	8,150					
Payments						
4 Supplies	2,500					
5 Wages	1,900					
6 Fuel	900					
7 Electricity	200					
8 Heating	200					
9 Rates	400					
10 Mortgage payment	900					
11 Interest on loan	450					
12 Total cash out (4 + 5 + 6… + 11)	7,450					
13 Net cash flow (3 − 12)	700					
14 Opening bank balance	(250)	450				
15 Closing bank balance (14 + 13)	450					

Figure 2.4 An example of a cash-flow forecast completed for the month of January

3.4 Why businesses forecast cash flow

Cash-flow forecasting is used to:

- forecast periods of time when cash outflows might exceed cash inflows, to allow entrepreneurs to take action (e.g. arranging a loan) in order to avoid the business being unable to pay bills when they become due
- plan when and how to finance major items of expenditure (e.g. vehicles or machinery), which may lead to large outflows of cash
- highlight any periods when cash surpluses may exist that could be more profitably invested elsewhere
- help entrepreneurs to assess whether their business idea is viable or whether it will not generate enough cash to be able to survive
- use as evidence with lenders (e.g. banks) that any loans given can and will be repaid

4 | *Setting budgets*

What you need to know:

- the structure of income, expenditure and profit budgets
- the process of setting budgets
- problems that may be encountered in setting budgets

4.1 The structure of income, expenditure and profit budgets

A **budget** is a financial plan. Its purpose is to provide a target for entrepreneurs and managers as well as a basis for a later assessment of the performance of a business. A budget should have a specific purpose and must have a set of targets attached to it if it is to be of value.

Income budgets

These record expected earnings from sales and are sometimes called **sales budgets**. For a newly established business they will be based on the results of market research. Established businesses can also call upon past trading records to provide information for sales forecasts. Income budgets are normally drawn up for the next financial year, on a monthly basis, as shown in Table 2.2.

Expenditure budgets

This type of budget sets out the expected spending of a business, broken down into a number of categories. The precise nature of these categories will depend upon the type of business. A manufacturing business will have sections entitled 'Raw materials' or 'Components', whereas a service business may not. The categories in Table 2.2 may vary according to the type of business.

Profit (or loss) budgets

This budget is derived from the above two and is calculated by taking forecast expenditure (or costs) from forecast income from sales. Depending on the balance between expenditure and income, a loss or a profit may be forecast. It is not unusual for a new business to forecast (and actually make) a loss during its first period of trading.

Table 2.2 shows forecast income, expenditure and profit/loss for a newly established manufacturer of surfboards. This extract shows forecasts the first 3 months of trading.

	April (£)	May (£)	June (£)
Cash sales	10,215	15,960	17,500
Credit sales	0	0	4,125
Total sales	**10,215**	**15,960**	**21,625**
Purchases of raw materials and components	19,500	14,010	15,550
Interest payments	1,215	1,105	1,350
Wages and salaries	3,000	2,850	2,995
Marketing and administration	2,450	2,400	2,450
Other costs	975	1,100	1,075
Total costs	**27,140**	**21,465**	**23,420**
Profit/(loss)	**(16,925)**	**(5,505)**	**(1,795)**

Table 2.2 Viking Boards Ltd's budget (April to June)

Examiner's tip

In an examination, you should be able to complete budgets such as the one above by inserting any missing figures, or be able to recalculate it if, for example, there is a change in the forecast income from sales.

4.2 The process of setting budgets

As Table 2.2 shows, budgets have a common structure. The top of the budget shows income, and this is followed by expenditure and finally by profit or loss. This is also the sequence in which budgets are set. Figure 2.5 summarises the process.

Entrepreneurs set budgets because:
- They are an essential element of a business plan. A bank is unlikely to grant a loan without evidence of this particular form of financial planning.
- Budgets can help entrepreneurs to decide whether or not to go ahead with a business idea. If the budget suggests that the business is going to incur a significant loss in its first year of trading, with little improvement evident, then a decision may be taken not to go ahead with the business.

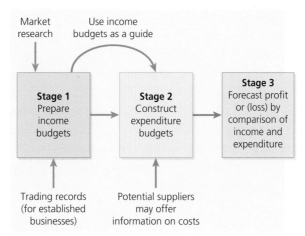

Figure 2.5 The process of setting budgets

- Budgets can help with pricing decisions. If a large loss is forecast, the entrepreneur may decide to sell the product at a higher price to improve the business's financial prospects.

4.3 Problems that may be encountered in setting budgets

The owner of a new business can expect to face several difficulties when drawing up a first set of budgets:

- There is no historical evidence available to assist a new enterprise in setting budgets. A new business has no trading records to show the level of sales income it received in previous years and perhaps how its sales income fluctuated throughout the year.
- Forecasting costs can also be problematic. The entrepreneur may lack the experience to estimate costs such as those for raw materials or wages.
- Competitors may respond to the appearance of a new business by cutting prices or promoting their products heavily. This can affect the sales income of the new business, as it may receive less than it forecast. In addition, the new business may have to engage in more promotion than expected, driving up its expenditure.

5 Assessing business start-ups

What you need to know:
- the objectives of business start-ups
- how to assess the strengths and weaknesses of a business plan or idea
- why start-ups can be risky
- why start-up businesses may fail

5.1 The objectives of business start-ups

A business **objective** is a medium- to long-term target or goal of an enterprise. It is often expressed in a quantified form. There are a number of reasons why people start their own businesses:

- **To develop an idea.** An entrepreneur may also be an inventor and have developed an idea for a good or service which they want to sell commercially. Crewe-based entrepreneur James Halliburton developed a tiny flotation device to prevent sailors and others losing valuable items, such as car keys and mobile phones, in the water. James established Seatriever International Ltd to manufacture and sell his invention.
- **To run a business.** Some people aspire to be their own boss and thereby to have greater control over their lives and not to be answerable to other people. This can be a powerful motivator for some would-be entrepreneurs.
- **To make money.** Surprisingly, research suggests that this not the most common objective among entrepreneurs when starting a business. Obviously some entrepreneurs do establish businesses with this objective, but it is likely to prove to be a very long-term objective. Many entrepreneurs do not become very wealthy, and of those who do, most achieve this only after many years of hard work.
- **To help society.** Some enterprises are established with the intention of helping the community in which the entrepreneur lives. This help may take the form of offering training and work to the unemployed, providing services to those who are disadvantaged, such as the disabled, or protecting the environment. Businesses established with this objective are often referred to as social enterprises. You can find out more about this type of business at **www.socialenterprise.org.uk**.

5.2 How to assess the strengths and weaknesses of a business plan or idea

Potential investors and suppliers as well as the entrepreneurs themselves are likely to have to assess the strengths and weaknesses of a business plan. What they look for may depend on the reason for their interest, but a number of common questions may be asked:

- **Will people buy the business's product?** This is of fundamental importance because if consumers do not want to buy the business's product, the enterprise will fail, irrespective of any other factors. Some entrepreneurs develop clever ideas, but these cannot be translated into commercial products. A shrewd assessor will look for evidence of appropriate and good quality primary research to provide evidence on the likelihood of the product proving popular with consumers. He or she will also look for some assessment of the competition and how the business plans to compete with these rivals.

- **Will the business make a profit?** It is perhaps unrealistic to expect a new enterprise to make an immediate profit; in fact, many new businesses start by incurring losses. However, it is likely that investors will look for evidence that the business will make a profit over the course of several years and so offer the prospect of a good return on the proposed investment. Evidence may be found in the form of sales forecasts and estimates of future profits.

- **Will the business run out of cash?** The lack of an adequate cash flow is a major problem for many start-up businesses. It may be that suppliers want to be paid on delivery, as they have no experience of trading with this business, while the entrepreneur may have to offer customers trade credit to attract them. Anyone analysing a business plan will look closely at a cash-flow forecast to judge its likely accuracy and also at plans in hand to deal with any cash-flow problems.

- **Does the plan fit together?** It is vital that the elements of a business plan are consistent. Do the cash-flow forecasts and forecast profit or loss match the sales forecasts and are they consistent with the results of market research?

5.3 Why start-ups can be risky

The risks facing a start-up business can be categorised as shown below, but they are all interdependent. Thus, for example, a threat to a business that originates in a change in the market (the emergence of a new competitor) can become a financial risk (falling sales revenue) very quickly.

Market-based risks

These can take a number of forms. There might be a change in the pattern of demand which leads to a decline in sales. At the time of writing, there is much speculation that the UK is heading into a recession (a period of 6 months or more when the economy does not grow, but becomes smaller). This has led to extreme difficulties for small businesses selling products such as new houses, luxury holidays and jewellery.

Changes in the market can cause other problems for businesses. A fall in price of the product can ruin financial forecasts, while sales forecasts may be wildly inaccurate if a health scare occurs or a new and improved product enters the market. A new business may find difficulty in attracting sufficient customers. Even if its primary market research suggested that people would buy its products, it can be difficult persuading people to change suppliers.

Financial risks

The major financial risk for most new businesses is a shortage of funds — both short term and long term. New businesses may not have sufficient capital to, for example, find a suitable location for the business. In the case of retailers, this can pose a significant threat to the business's survival. Equally, a shortage of cash (possibly because customers are slow in paying) may mean that the start-up business struggles to pay its own suppliers. Failure to meet their payment terms may result in the closure of the business. Banks may be unwilling to lend money to new businesses with a very limited trading record.

Operating risks

These can take a number of forms. Breakdowns, late deliveries, substandard supplies, unreliable employees, and safety or security problems can all prevent the production process taking place, or taking place in time to meet customer needs. These risks are much more real for a new business that does not have customer goodwill, experience or extra cash resources to help overcome the possible problems.

Examiner's tip

Try to think about the likely causes of risk or failure in the context of the business that you are considering. So, for example, a manufacturing business that has to buy raw materials and may take time to convert them into a finished product is more likely to suffer from cash-flow problems. Alternatively, a business selling luxury products is more vulnerable to a slowdown in the economy and a reduction in consumer spending.

5.4 Why start-up businesses may fail

The reasons why start-up businesses are risky are also largely the reasons why they fail. A high proportion of start-up businesses do not survive the first 3 years of trading. Research by Barclays Bank revealed that nearly 50% of the businesses that started during the financial year 2001/02 were not trading in 2005.

The precise causes of failure vary according to the type of start-up business and the market in which it is trading. Nevertheless there are a number of common causes of failure:

- **Lack of management skills and experience.** Many people who manage a start-up business have not done so before. They lack experience and may not recognise the first signs of impending problems or, if they do, they may take inappropriate action or possibly no action at all. New managers may not be able to get the best out of their employees or have the necessary skills to negotiate favourable deals with suppliers and customers. They may not have the necessary contacts in the business world to seek advice and help when things go badly.
- **Insufficient demand.** Market research is not always reliable and it is easy for entrepreneurs to interpret it positively when they are keen to get their new enterprise established. However, it is a common experience of entrepreneurs to discover that sales (perhaps after an initial boom) are below expectations. In these circumstances, they may be forced to cut prices, which can in itself be a threat to the business's survival.

- **Cash-flow problems.** Many managers are unaware of the importance of cash flow and of how difficult it can be to manage it successfully in a start-up business. Research has shown that cash-flow problems cause the demise of many businesses, not only those that have recently been established.
- **Unexpected events.** The slowdown in spending in the economy due to the 'credit crunch' of 2008 led to an 8.5% rise in the number of small businesses failing in the UK. While not all of these were start-up businesses, it does indicate the impact that an unexpected event can have on the survival chances of vulnerable small businesses. Other unexpected events might include changes in tastes or fashions and the innovation of new products.

1 General advice in preparing for Unit 1

1.1 The examination

This unit is assessed through a mini case study on which short-answer and extended questions are based. The case study tells the story of a start-up business using text, numbers and diagrams as necessary. Key facts relating to this examination are as follows:

- Duration: 1 hour and 15 minutes.
- Total marks available: 60.
- Weighting of the examination: 40% of AS; 20% of A-level.
- Available: January and June from January 2009.

The Unit 1 examination is presented in three distinct sections:

- **The case.** This sets out the story of planning a new business. The enterprise could be based in any section of the economy (primary, secondary or tertiary) and could be a franchise. However, it will be a small business.
- **Section A.** This comprises a number of questions requiring short answers, such as definitions or calculations. These questions will test knowledge as well as the skill of application.
- **Section B.** This comprises a number of questions requiring extended responses, which will also test the skills of analysis and evaluation.

A copy of AQA's specimen Unit 1 paper and the marking scheme can be found at:
www.aqa.org.uk/qual/gce/pdf/business_studies_new.php

1.2 How to prepare for the examination

This examination is revision-intensive. That means that you have to master all of the Unit 1 specification to make sure that you are able to answer all the questions that are asked on the examination paper. In particular, the first section will ask a series of small questions ranging over the entire Unit 1 specification. You can be sure that it will reveal any gaps in your subject knowledge. You should make sure that you can define all the terms that are listed in the specification and that you are able to carry out relevant calculations, such as market share and growth, profits (or losses) and breakeven. In the Unit 1 examination, 35% of the marks (21 out of the 60 available) are for demonstrating relevant knowledge.

The examination tests other skills too.

Application

Application is the skill of applying your answers to the context set out in the examination paper. This is an important skill in Unit 1 and is worth 25% of the marks available on the paper. Unit 1 will provide you with a lot of information about a particular business, some of which may be in numerical form. It is essential that you relate your answers to this business and avoid discussing businesses in general or, worse still, another business. The examiner has included hooks for you to pick up on. He or she may have said that the business has forecast cash-flow problems or that the entrepreneur has absolutely no experience of running a business. These are things that you can use in your answers to gain application marks.

Analysis

Analysis is developing a line of argument and following it through. It commonly focuses on causes or effects or on interrelationships. The word 'why' is helpful in encouraging you to write analytically. Thus, if you were arguing that a potential cause of failure for a specific start-up business was a lack of cash, you would gain analysis marks for explaining why this was so. Analysis carries the same proportion of marks as application in Unit 1: 25%. Questions requiring analysis use verbs (or command words) such as 'analyse' and 'examine'.

Evaluation

This is the skill of judgement. Questions in Unit 1 calling for evaluation carry high mark allocations (approximately between 13 and 17 marks). You can recognise this type of question by command words such as 'discuss', 'evaluate', 'to what extent' and 'justify'. Good evaluation often builds on the skill of application by making judgements about the specific business in the case, rather than businesses in general. Good evaluation makes a clear judgement and supports it.

2   *A sample Unit 1 examination paper*

Going ashore

Jim Trevelyan's decision to sell his fishing boat and open a fresh-fish shop seemed to be a good one. He had found the demands of inshore fishing increasingly tiring and wanted to spend more time in his beautiful house overlooking the sea in Southwold, a wealthy town on the Suffolk coast.

Jim had the skills necessary to manage his new business successfully. He liked being in charge and making decisions, but he was not good at listening to other people's views. He was knowledgeable about fish and understood how to manage a business, so he did not conduct primary research. He had plenty of contacts in the business and had sold fish directly to restaurants in Suffolk, earning a reputation for selling high-quality products.

He spent the first few weeks researching and planning his proposed business. His idea was simple. He intended to use the money raised from selling his boat to purchase a suitable property to use as a fish shop in Southwold, which he knew well and liked living in. Once this property was refurbished and ready, he would start buying fish daily from Lowestoft, a few miles away. Although Jim wished to sell fish to as many people as possible, he intended engage in market segmentation and to target high-income earners in particular.

He faced no local competition for selling fresh fish in the Southwold area — the only other fish shop closed 1 year ago. Jim was confident that he would be able to purchase high-quality produce from the local fishermen and develop a reputation for supplying a quality product. Thus he could attract high-income customers (including restaurants) willing to pay premium prices.

Jim had much of the finance needed for his fish shop — £175,000 from selling his boat. Despite this, he still needed to raise some finance to carry out his plans. Jim estimated that he would need £50,000, which he decided to raise by taking on another shareholder and forming a private limited company. Jim was experienced enough to know that the first few months of trading could be a difficult period.

Jim's business planning had progressed — he thought his business would not be risky. He had investigated his likely expenditure during his first year of trading as thoroughly as possible.

This information allowed him to estimate his total costs and, when put alongside his forecast sales, gave an estimated profit figure for the first year of Jim's fish shop. This information is shown in **Appendix A**. Jim was very keen that his new business should make a profit as soon as possible.

Jim's business experience had told him how important it was for new businesses to manage cash flow carefully. He had drawn up his cash-flow forecast for the first year of trading and was surprised to see that he was likely to face problems during the year. The early months looked like they would be the most difficult, as he would have to pay for the property, decorating and fitting it out, as well as some legal costs. The first 4 months of Jim's cash-flow forecast are shown in **Appendix B**.

Appendix A: Jim's forecast costs and revenues data

Item	£
Fixed costs for the year	18,500
Monthly variable costs (average)	2,450
Sales revenue per month (average)	5,125

Appendix B: Jim's cash-flow forecast

	October	November	December	January
Sales	1,160	2,325	3,650	4,000
Capital introduced	175,400	50,000	0	0
Total cash Inflow	**176,560**	**52,325**	**3,650**	**4,000**
Purchase and refitting of shop	229,500	2,400	0	0
Purchases of fish	450	780	900	845
Interest payments	0	640	640	640
Wages	1,000	1,000	1,250	1,000
Other costs (e.g. advertising)	3,980	1,805	2,100	750
Total cash outflow	**234,930**	**6,625**	**4,890**	**3,235**
Net cash flow	**(58,370)**	**45,700**	**(1,240)**	**765**
Opening balance	3,200	(55,170)	(9,470)	(10,710)
Closing balance	(55,170)	(9,470)	(10,710)	(9,945)

Question 1

(a) What is meant by the term 'cash flow'? (2 marks)

(b) What is meant by the term 'market segmentation'? (2 marks)

(c) Calculate Jim's forecast monthly profit using the information in Appendix A. (5 marks)

(d) Assume that Jim's cash inflow in January is 25% higher than he had forecast in Appendix B and that his total wages are £1,200 for that month. Recalculate the following for **January** only in the light of these changes:
(i) cash outflow
(ii) net cash flow
(iii) closing balance (5 marks)

(e) Explain two possible sources of information that Jim might use in constructing his business plan. (6 marks)

Total for question 1: 20 marks

Question 2

(a) Analyse the factors that may have influenced Jim to locate his fish shop in Southwold. (10 marks)

(b) Should Jim operate his business as a sole trader or as a private limited company? You should justify your view. (13 marks)

(c) To what extent do you think that Jim's business would be a risky venture? (17 marks)

Total for question 2: 40 marks

Unit 2

Managing a business

CHAPTER 4 Finance

1 Using budgets

What you need to know:
- the benefits and drawbacks of using budgets
- how to calculate and interpret variances
- how to use variances to inform decision making

1.1 The benefits and drawbacks of using budgets

The detail and the content of the budget should be the result of negotiation with all concerned. Those responsible for keeping to a budget should play a part in setting it, if it is to work as an effective motivator.

Benefits of budgets

Using budgets offers several benefits:
- Targets can be set for each section, allowing management to identify the extent to which each section contributes to the overall objectives of the business.
- Attention is drawn to inefficiency and waste, so that appropriate remedial action can be taken.
- Budgets make managers think about the financial implications of their actions and focus decision making on the achievement of targets and corporate objectives.
- Budgeting should improve financial control, if only because employees are aware that their actions are being scrutinised.
- Budgets can help improve internal communication.
- Delegated or devolved budgets can be used as a motivator by giving employees authority and the opportunity to fulfil some of their higher-level needs, as identified by Maslow (see pages 65–66). At the same time, senior managers can retain control of the business by monitoring budgets.

Drawbacks of budgets

The use of budgets can lead to the following disadvantages:
- The operation of budgets can become inflexible. For example, sales may be lost if the marketing budget is strictly adhered to at a time when competitors are undertaking major promotional campaigns.
- Budgets have to be reasonably accurate to have any meaning. Wide differences (or variances) between budgeted and actual figures can demotivate staff and call the whole process into question.

1.2 How to calculate and interpret variances

Variance analysis is the study by managers of the differences between planned activities in the form of budgets and the actual results that were achieved. Table 4.1 is an example of a monthly budget for a restaurant.

As the period covered by the budget unfolds, actual results can be compared with the budgeted figures and variances examined.

A **positive (or favourable) variance** occurs when costs are lower than forecast or profit or revenues higher, as in the case of sales revenue and profits in Table 4.1.

A **negative (or adverse) variance** arises when costs are higher than expected or revenues are less than anticipated. Examples are wage costs and food and drink in Table 4.1.

Item	Budget figure (£)	Actual figure (£)	Variance (£)
Sales revenue	39,500	42,420	2,920 (favourable)
Fixed costs	9,500	9,500	0
Wages costs	10,450	11,005	555 (adverse)
Food and drink	8,475	9,826	1,351 (adverse)
Other costs	5,300	6,000	700 (adverse)
Total costs	33,725	36,331	2,606 (adverse)
Profit/loss	5,775	6,089	314 (favourable)

Table 4.1 An example of calculating variances

1.3 How to use variances to inform decision making

Positive variances might occur because of good budgetary control or by accident: for example, due to rising market prices.

Possible responses to positive variances are:
- to increase production if prices are rising, giving increased profit margins
- to reduce prices if costs are below expectation and the business aims to increase its sales and market share
- to increase investment into the business or pay shareholders increased dividends if profits exceed expectations

Negative variances might occur due to inadequate control or factors outside the firm's control, such as rising raw material costs.

Possible responses to negative variances are:
- to reduce costs (e.g. by buying less expensive materials) to help to control costs
- to increase advertising in order to increase sales of the product and revenues
- to reduce prices to increase sales (relies on demand being price elastic)

The key issue about using the results of variance analysis to help decision making is to take into account the causes of the adverse or favourable variances. Just because a result is favourable does not mean that everything is in order. Neither does an adverse variance mean that the area responsible has been inefficient. A favourable production material variance could be generated from using lower-quality raw materials, which in turn could manifest itself as a drop in sales. Similarly, an adverse cost variance may occur because sales are higher than forecast and the business has incurred extra costs in supplying customers' demands.

Examiner's tip

Look for the relationships between revenues, costs and profits when considering variances. For example, if sales revenue has recorded a negative variance, it would be reasonable to expect costs, especially variable costs, to show a positive variance. If they do not, profits are likely to have a negative variance.

2 *Improving cash flow*

What you need to know:
- the causes of cash-flow problems
- the methods of improving cash flow

2.1 The causes of cash-flow problems

Cash-flow problems can have a number of causes:
- **Poor management of cash flow.** If managers do not forecast and monitor the business's cash flow, problems are more likely to arise and more likely to lead to a serious financial situation. Similarly, the failure to chase up customers who owe the company money can lead to lower inflows and possible cash shortages.
- **Giving too much trade credit.** When a firm offers trade credit, it gives its customers time to settle their accounts — this might be 30, 60 or 90 days. In effect, this is an interest-free loan and while it helps to attract customers it slows down the business's cash inflows, thereby reducing its cash balance.
- **Overtrading.** This happens when a business expands rapidly without planning how to finance the expansion. An expanding business has to pay for materials and labour in advance of receiving the cash inflow from sales. A growing business does this on an increasing scale and may struggle to fund its expenditure.
- **Unexpected expenditure.** A business may incur unexpected costs, resulting in a cash outflow. The breakdown of a machine or a substantial rise in wages can lead to significant outflows of cash, weakening the enterprise's cash position.

2.2 The methods of improving cash flow

There are several methods of improving cash flow.

Factoring

This is particularly useful for small businesses, which may experience difficulty in controlling credit. Factoring enables a business to sell its outstanding debtors to a specialist debt collector called a **factor**. The business receives approximately 80% of the value of the debt immediately. The factor then receives payment of the bill from the customer and passes on the balance to the firm, holding back about 5% to cover expenses. This enables the business to improve cash flow considerably, as it does not have to wait for payment. Factoring does, however, reduce profit margins, as approximately 5% of revenue is 'lost'.

Sale and leaseback

This is a distinctive form of finance whereby the owner of an asset sells it and then leases it back. It provides a short-term boost to the business's finances, as the sale of the asset generates revenue. However, the business commits itself to paying rent for the asset for the foreseeable future.

Improved working capital control

This can help cash-flow management by:
- enabling lower stocks to be held, thus making more liquid assets available
- improving debtor control, ensuring that debtors do not overextend their credit terms, or allowing shorter credit periods (but this could have an impact on sales)
- lengthening supplier credit terms to allow finances to remain under the company's control for longer

Other possibilities are:

- stimulating sales, by offering discounts for cash and prompt payment
- selling off excess material stocks
- taking on additional long-term loans to improve the short-term cash position

3 *Measuring and increasing profit*

What you need to know:

- how to calculate and understand profit margins
- how to calculate and understand return on capital
- the methods of improving profits and profitability
- the distinction between cash flow and profit

3.1 How to calculate and understand profit margins

Profit is a major objective for many businesses, but not for all businesses. Social enterprises, for example, pursue other targets such as helping the disadvantaged in society. It is simplistic to say that a business that makes a larger profit than another business is achieving a higher level of performance. It may be that the business generating the higher profits is much larger. To make a profit figure more meaningful, it needs to be compared to something else.

The **net profit margin** is a ratio that calculates the business's profit after the deduction of all costs as a percentage of its revenue from sales.

$$\text{net profit margin} = \frac{\text{net profit}}{\text{sales revenue}} \times 100$$

A business can calculate a profit margin for a single product or for all of its production. Table 4.2 shows examples of both of these methods of calculation.

Units sold	Sales revenue (£)	Total costs (£)	Profit (£)	Net profit margin (%)
24,500	232,750	200,165	32,585	14.0
1	9.50	8.17	1.33	14.0

Table 4.2 Net profit margin for a single product or for a business's entire output

Higher profit margins are better than lower ones. A higher profit margin gives a business a greater level of overall profit and allows it to reward its owners more fully or to invest in improving its scale or efficiency.

Examiner's tip

Always show your workings when calculating a profit margin. In the event of making an arithmetical error, you will still receive some of the marks available. If an examination paper includes a firm's profit margin, do not ignore it. Try to use it to develop an argument in answer to one of the questions.

Profit margins vary according to the type of business. Food retailers seek to sell food quickly and will accept a relatively low profit margin (Tesco's is around 6%) because they sell a large volume of products. In contrast, other retailers that sell more expensive products less frequently might seek a much higher profit margin. Thus, a jeweller would expect a much higher profit margin than Tesco.

3.2 How to calculate and understand return on capital

Profits are the result of an investment by the owners of a business. One means of judging the profitability of a business is to compare the amount of profit to the investment that was needed to start the enterprise or project.

The formula to calculate return on capital is:

$$\text{return on capital} = \frac{\text{net profit}}{\text{capital investment}} \times 100$$

Assume an entrepreneur sets up a business by investing £250,000, and in a given year the business generates a net profit of £12,500. The return on capital in these circumstances would be £12,500/£250,000 × 100 = 5%.

Once again a higher figure is preferable. However, it is advisable to look at the return over a number of years. In particular, a newly established business will take time to build up a customer base and it is likely that its return on capital will improve over time. It is often true that businesses with high returns on capital are also risky. It is wise to judge the return on capital against the degree of risk. Finally, do take opportunity cost into account. In what other ways could this capital have been invested? A safer use with a slightly lower return might be a wiser use of the capital.

3.3 The methods of improving profits and profitability

Profits are simply a figure that measures the amount by which a business's sales revenue exceeds its total costs. Profitability measures profits against some yardstick, such as the sales revenue achieved by the business.

Firms can increase their profits by taking a variety of actions:
- **Increasing prices.** An increase in price has the potential to increase revenue without raising total costs. However, this is a risky strategy because an increase in price may result in a large fall in sales. In this situation, the result may be a decrease in profits if the fall in sales more than offsets the increase in price per unit. The extent to which this happens depends upon price elasticity of demand (see pages 92–93 for more details on price elasticity).
- **Cutting costs.** Lowering costs of production can increase the profit margin, as it should result in a higher profit margin. But this may be at the expense of quality. A decline in quality could have an adverse effect on the quantity of sales as well as the firm's reputation.
- **Using its capacity as fully as possible.** If a business has productive capacity that is not being utilised, its profits will be lower than they might otherwise be. If train companies run services that are only 50% occupied, their revenue is much lower. Offering deals and incentives to customers to use the trains could increase profits significantly, as it costs little more to run a full train than a half-full one.
- **Increasing efficiency.** Avoiding waste in the form of poor quality and unsaleable products, using staff as fully as possible and using a minimal amount of resources to make products are all ways of improving the efficiency of a business. Improving efficiency is likely to result in increased profits.

3.4 The distinction between cash flow and profit

It is important to understand that cash flow and profit are very different concepts.

Profit, at its simplest, is the surplus of revenues over total costs, over some defined period of time. If a business earns revenues of £2 million during a financial year and incurs total costs of £1.5 million, it will generate profits of £0.5 million.

Cash flow relates to the timing of inflows and outflows of cash to and from a business. The profitable business referred to in the previous paragraph might experience cash-flow problems for a number of reasons. The two listed below are arguably the most important:

- **If its customers are slow to pay.** This delays its cash inflows and may lead to it having difficulty in settling its own bills as they fall due. This can become a major concern if the business does not chase up its customers and require them to pay.
- **If it offers long periods of trade credit.** Giving customers 30 or 60 days to settle their accounts may help to increase sales but can result in a shortage of cash when it is needed.

Thus profitable businesses can face cash-flow difficulties if they do not manage their cash effectively.

1 Improving organisational structures

What you need to know:
● the key elements of an organisational structure
● the major workforce roles
● how organisational structure affects business performance

1.1 The key elements of an organisational structure

An organisational structure shows how roles in a particular enterprise are arranged to allow the business to perform its commercial activities. The organisational structure establishes the relationships between the different components of the organisation, including its lines of communication and authority.

Levels of hierarchy

The **level of hierarchy** refers to the number of layers of authority in an organisation. In the past, many organisations were tall, with many layers of hierarchy, and were often authoritarian. Figure 5.1 shows an organisation with four levels of hierarchy. This would be referred to as a relatively 'flat' organisation.

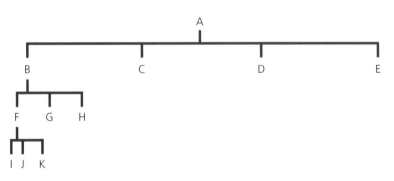

Figure 5.1 Hierarchies and spans of control

Spans of control

The **span of control** is the number of subordinates for whom a manager is directly responsible. In Figure 5.1, manager A has a span of control of 4 because he or she is not directly responsible for employees F, G, H, I, J and K. Employee B has a span of control of 3. The maximum recommended span for effective management is 6, although this is regularly exceeded, particularly in recent years. The span of control in operation will depend upon a number of factors:
● The experience and personality of the manager.
● The nature of the business. If being a line manager requires a great deal of close supervision, a narrower span might be appropriate.
● The skills and attitudes of the employees. Highly skilled, professional employees might flourish in a business adopting wide spans of control.
● The tradition of the organisation. A business with a tradition of democratic management and empowered workers may operate wider spans of control.

Workloads and job allocations

Workload refers to the number of duties that an employee is expected to carry out. From the point of view of managers, it is cost effective to require employees to carry out the maximum number of duties. It is common for the owners of small and medium-sized businesses to work very long hours to try to make the enterprise successful. Some entrepreneurs expect employees to show similar levels of commitment and this may result in very long working weeks. In some businesses, the workload may vary according to the time of year. The workloads of people employed in agriculture are likely to be higher in the summer months, for example.

Job allocation is a term used to describe the way in which the organisation's duties are divided among the different employees in the business. In a newly established small business, it is common for employees to carry out a wide range of duties. In part this may be because the business is unable to afford to hire specialist staff to carry out particular tasks. As a business grows, it may hire specialist employees and the job allocations of individual employees may become less varied.

Delegation

Delegation can be defined as the passing of authority to a subordinate within the organisation. Although a task may be passed down from a superior to a subordinate, the manager still has responsibility for making sure that the job is completed. On the other hand, **authority** is the power to carry out the task. It is possible to delegate authority, but responsibility remains with the delegator.

To delegate, a manager must trust the delegatee and it is important that the subordinate feels that trust is placed in him or her. A prudent manager will also want to exercise some control over the subordinate — for example, via reports and inspections. Any increase in control exercised by the manager decreases the amount of trust enjoyed by the subordinate. The use of delegation has implications for the workloads of both parties involved.

Communication flows

Communication is the exchange of information or ideas between two or more parties. For a business to operate effectively, it is important that effective communication takes places throughout the entire organisation.

Figure 5.2 shows that communication flows can be:
- upward (from junior to more senior employees)
- sideways or horizontal (between employees in the same level of hierarchy of the organisation)
- downwards from senior to junior employees

It is also important that communication is two-way. This allows the sender of the communication to confirm that the message has been understood and enables the recipient to raise any necessary queries.

1.2 Workforce roles

A workforce comprises employees whose roles can be categorised in a number of ways. One possible classification is set out below.
- **Shop-floor employees.** Shop-floor employees carry out basic duties in an organisation. They may be clerks in an office, assistants in a shop or teaching assistants in a school. They are at the bottom of the organisational structure and are not responsible for other employees.
- **Supervisors or team leaders.** Supervisors provide a link between managers and shop-floor workers, and have responsibility for a group of employees. They may also have the authority to take certain decisions on routine issues such as staff rotas. Team

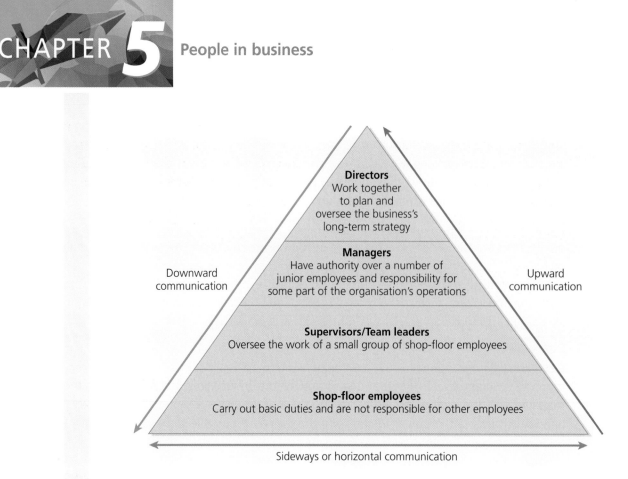

Figure 5.2 *Workforce roles and communication flows*

leaders carry out a similar role, but in an organisation that relies heavily on delegation they are more likely to work alongside shop-floor workers.

- **Managers.** Managers are responsible for organising others in the business and usually have some responsibility for a particular aspect of the business's operations. Managers in many organisations have to plan, organise, motivate and control.
- **Directors.** Directors are elected by the shareholders of the company and work together as a team: the **board of directors**. The directors set out the main aims of the business and monitor the strategies that the business adopts to try to meet its aims. Full-time or executive directors, such as the finance director, are responsible for important divisions or departments within the business. Part-time or non-executive directors are normally appointed because they bring some particular expertise to the business.

1.3 How organisational structure affects business performance

Small and medium-sized businesses seek an organisational structure that allows the business to:
- operate as efficiently as possible
- operate flexibly as the enterprise grows and/or changes

An efficient organisational structure can help a business to use its human resources as effectively as possible. The efficient use of employees means that they should have a workload which is manageable, and this should encourage high levels of motivation and productivity. In service industries such as hotels and restaurants, this can assist a business in providing high levels of customer service. The organisational structure should also be structured to employ people in ways that allow them to use their skills. These skills might relate to a function, such as financial or marketing skills, or be more generic management skills.

However, an organisational structure is likely to change over time, particularly if a business is growing. Developing more levels of hierarchy or appointing more people at particular levels in the hierarchy can help the organisation to be responsive and prevent people overworking, with possible consequent damage to the individual's performance. If managers are aware of the relationships between organisational structure and the performance of the business, it is likely that they will allow the structure to evolve in order to provide a responsive and efficient service to customers.

Measuring the effectiveness of the workforce

What you need to know:
- methods of measuring workforce performance
- how to interpret the results

2.1 Methods of measuring the effectiveness of the workforce

Managers need to measure employee performance in an objective way for the following reasons:
- to assess the efficiency (and competitiveness) of the workforce
- to assist in developing the workforce plan
- to confirm that the business's human resource planning is contributing directly to the achievement of corporate objectives

The performance of employees helps to identify the need for training, further recruitment or, perhaps, redundancy or redeployment. There are a number of ways in which a business can assess the performance of its current labour force.

Labour productivity

$$\text{labour productivity} = \frac{\text{output per period}}{\text{number of employees at work}} \times 100$$

If employees are producing a similar or greater amount each day, week or month than employees of rival businesses, then productivity may be satisfactory. However, such comparisons may be simplistic: factors such as wage rates, the level of technology and the way the labour force is organised will also be important.

Labour turnover

$$\text{labour turnover (\%)} = \frac{\text{number of staff leaving during the year}}{\text{average number of staff}} \times 100$$

A high level of labour turnover could be caused by many factors:
- inadequate wage levels, leading employees to defect to competitors
- poor morale and low levels of motivation within the workforce
- the selection of the wrong employees in the first place, meaning they leave to seek more suitable employment
- a buoyant local labour market, offering more (and perhaps more attractive) opportunities to employees

2.2 How to interpret the results

In general, higher rates of productivity are preferable to lower rates. Higher rates of productivity can, in effect, reduce the costs of production, allowing a business to charge lower prices or to enjoy higher profit margins. However, if high levels of productivity are achieved at the expense of quality and therefore customer satisfaction, any gains may exist only in the short term.

High rates of labour turnover are expensive in terms of additional recruitment costs, lost production and the damage that may be done to morale and productivity. On the other hand, some level of labour turnover is important to bring new ideas, skills and enthusiasm to the labour force.

Examiner's tip

It is important to look behind any labour force data with which you are provided. For example, two sets of productivity data may suggest that firm A has a clear advantage. This may become less clear cut when the following factors relating to firm B are taken into account.
- Wage rates are significantly lower.
- Morale is excellent.
- A training programme is being implemented, causing short-term disruption.
- There is a low incidence of industrial relations problems.
- A reputation for craftsmanship and quality products has been established.

3 Developing an effective workforce: recruitment, selection, training

What you need to know:
- the recruitment process
- internal and external recruitment
- selecting the best employees
- how recruitment and selection can improve a workforce
- methods of training

3.1 The recruitment process

Recruitment is the finding and appointment of new employees.

All businesses, even very small ones, need to recruit employees at some stage. The recruitment process is shown in Figure 5.3.

Recruitment documentation
The necessary documentation for the recruitment process is shown below.

Job adverts contain the following information:
- job title
- some description of duties
- location
- name of the business
- possibly salary and working hours

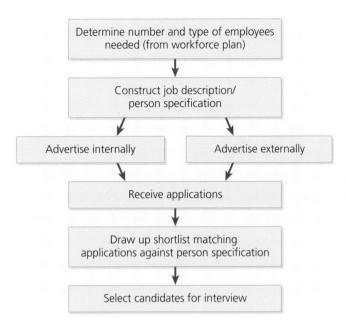

Figure 5.3 The process of recruitment

The advert may be local for a relatively unskilled job. Highly skilled and professional positions might require advertising nationally or even internationally.

Job descriptions may act as the basis for drawing up the advert for the post and relate to the position rather than the person. Typically, job descriptions contain the following information:
- title of the post
- employment conditions
- some idea of tasks and duties
- to whom employees are responsible
- likely targets and standards that employees are expected to meet

Person or job specifications set out the qualifications and qualities required of an employee. The list might include:
- educational and professional qualifications required
- character and personality traits expected
- physical characteristics needed
- experience necessary

Recruitment can be an expensive exercise but is less costly than appointing the wrong employee and perhaps having to repeat the process.

3.2 Internal and external recruitment

Recruitment may take place either internally or externally.

Internal recruitment

Firms may recruit internally through promotion or redeployment of existing employees. This offers several benefits:
- It is cheaper, as it avoids the need for expensive external advertising.
- Candidates will have experience of the business and may not require induction training.
- Selection may be easier, as more is known about the candidates.

However, problems exist in recruiting internally:

- Selection is from a smaller pool of available labour and the calibre of candidates may be lower. This can be significant for senior appointments.
- Difficulties can result if employees are promoted from within — former colleagues may resent taking orders from those whom they formerly worked alongside.

External recruitment

Managers may be keen to have a wider choice of candidates and therefore advertise externally. The advantages of this approach are as follows:

- It is likely that higher-quality candidates will be available following external recruitment, even if advertisements are only placed in local media.
- External candidates will bring fresh ideas and enthusiasm into the business.

But again drawbacks exist:

- It is more expensive to recruit externally, especially if national advertising or employment agencies are used.
- The degree of risk is greater, even if extensive selection processes are used, as candidates are less known to the business.

Examiner's tip

Students sometimes provide huge amounts of information on recruitment and selection. This is primarily a descriptive area and one on which relatively straightforward questions testing knowledge and understanding are normally set. Few marks are normally available for such questions. It is more important to appreciate the role of recruitment and selection within the whole human resource management process and the influences on this process.

3.3 Selecting the best employees

Because of the costs involved in recruiting the wrong people, firms are investing more resources and time in the recruitment process. Although effective selection techniques may be expensive, they are considerably cheaper than appointing the wrong employee.

A range of selection techniques exist:

- **Interviews** remain the most common form of selection and may involve one or two interviewers or even a panel interview. Interviews are relatively cheap and allow the two-way exchange of information, but they are unreliable as a method of selection. Some people perform well at interview, but that does not necessarily mean they will perform well in the post.
- **Psychometric tests** reveal more about the personality of a candidate than might be discovered through interview. Questions are frequently used to assess candidates' management skills or their ability their to work within a team.
- **Aptitude tests** may provide an insight into a candidate's current ability and potential. Such tests can also be used to assess intelligence and job-related skills.
- **Assessment centres** expose candidates for jobs to a number of methods of selection, including role-plays, group activities and simulations of circumstances that might occur in the job. Assessment centres allow a direct comparison between candidates.

3.4 How recruitment and selection can improve a workforce

Appointing the wrong people can be very costly. First, while employed they may make errors (e.g. supplying the wrong products to particular customers or offering substandard service) which could result in the loss of sales and profits. In a highly competitive market, or for a business that is seeking growth, recruiting the wrong people can make it difficult, or even impossible, for a business to achieve its objectives.

There is a second consequence of appointing inappropriate employees. Recruitment is an expensive process. Costs are incurred in advertising positions (these costs can be high if national advertising is necessary) as well as in staff time spent selecting people to be interviewed and during the interview (or other selection) process. As senior employees may be involved in the selection process, the costs of their time can be high. A survey by *Personnel Today* has estimated that recruitment costs, excluding advertising costs, average over £5,000 per employee.

Recruitment can, however, be looked at in a more positive way. Appointing the right people to a business offers a range of benefits:
- Levels of productivity are likely to be high, improving the business's financial performance.
- If people are in the right job, they are likely to be able to make a greater contribution to the business by, for example, using their initiative.
- Recruiting the right people reduces the workload of their line managers, freeing them for other duties.
- Effective recruitment policies ultimately save time in terms of disciplining, dismissing and replacing people who do not perform well in their posts.

3.5 Methods of training

Training entails improving the skills and knowledge of the workforce. Almost all employees receive some training when they commence a particular job. This is known as **induction training**. Induction training is intended to introduce an employee to the business in which they will be working. It may include familiarisation with some or all of the following:
- important policies and procedures, such as appraisal, holiday entitlement, systems and disciplinary/grievance matters
- the layout of the factory or offices
- personnel with whom the new employee will be working
- health and safety and security procedures
- the fundamental duties associated with the job

Induction training offers a number of advantages to businesses:
- It enables a new recruit to become more productive more quickly.
- It can prevent costly errors resulting from employee ignorance.
- It may make a new employee feel more welcome and reduce labour turnover.

There are two broad types of training:
- **Off-the-job.** This is training outside the workplace, at a college, university or some other training agency, or at the employee's home. Off-the-job training can take the form of external courses, perhaps in the form of lectures and seminars, self-study or open learning.

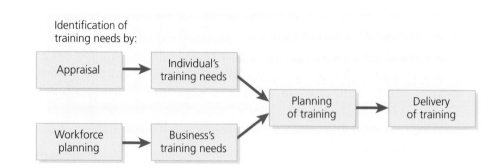

Figure 5.4 Training

- **On-the-job.** This form of training does not require the employee to leave the workplace. He or she learns from more experienced employees through observation and work shadowing. Alternatively, the trainee may work through instruction manuals, operate with a mentor or receive more formal guidance from senior employees.

The advantages and disadvantages of each type of training are shown in Table 5.1.

In spite of being expensive, and sometimes disruptive, training does offer organisations a number of benefits:

- Well-trained employees are likely to be better motivated, as they feel valued by their employers and get a sense of achievement from performing their work more efficiently or carrying out more complex duties.
- Training improves employee performance, resulting in a more productive and efficient workforce. This can improve the competitiveness of the organisation.
- Training can help to reduce labour turnover, as employees are more satisfied with their work. It may also help to make the business more attractive to potential employees.

The government encourages training through its 'Investors in People' scheme. Firms that meet the requirement for training employees (in particular, for training employees to assist in meeting corporate objectives) are entitled to use a logo identifying them as meeting the Investors in People standard. This may assist the business in its dealings

	Off-the-job	On-the-job
Advantages	• Employees are not distracted by work pressures. • Specialists can be used to provide training. • Often carries greater conviction with employees.	• Simple to organise and often relatively cheap. • Closely related to the needs and circumstances of the business. • Employees can see the relevance of the training.
Disadvantages	• Can be costly. • Employees absent from work for a period of time. • Can place greater pressures (extra hours, commitment) on other employees. • If general training, employees may leave when complete.	• Those delivering training often do not have teaching or training skills. • Trainees can be distracted by the demands of the job (e.g. by phone calls). • Training can be narrowly focused, not looking at the broader needs of the organisation.

Table 5.1 Advantages and disadvantages of training

with customers and other businesses. Indeed, some firms will only deal with suppliers if they have the Investors in People award.

4 Developing and retaining an effective workforce: motivating employees

What you need to know:

- theories of motivation
- the use of financial methods to motivate employees
- improving job design
- team working and empowerment

4.1 Theories of motivation

What is motivation?

Analysts disagree on the precise meaning of the term **motivation**. It can be defined as 'the will to work due to enjoyment of the work itself'. This suggests that motivation comes from within an individual employee. A different view of motivation is that it is the will or desire to achieve a given target or goal, due to some external stimulus. Many of the differences in the theories of motivation can be explained in terms of this fundamental difference of definition. Figure 5.5 shows the various schools of thought relating to motivation.

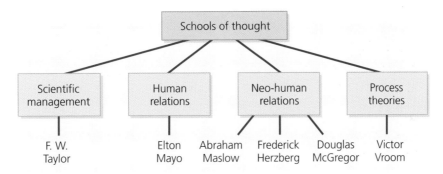

Figure 5.5 Schools of thought relating to motivation

Examiner's tip

You don't need to know any particular theory of motivation. The ones set out below are possibilities, although others would be equally suitable. However, you should aim to know at least one theory relating to financial methods of motivation and at least one theory relating to non-financial methods of motivation.

The school of scientific management

The first writings on motivating employees emerged in the latter stages of the nineteenth century.

Motivating workers became an important issue as the size of organisations increased and as the factory system became firmly entrenched in manufacturing processes. The development of mass production methods increased the number of people working in factories, while making their tasks more routine and monotonous. It therefore became an important element of the duties of management to motivate employees so as to improve competitiveness.

A 'school of thought' is simply a group of people who hold broadly similar views. The school of scientific management argues that business decisions should be taken on the basis of data that are researched and tested quantitatively. Members of the school believe that it is vital to identify ways in which costs can be accounted for precisely, so that efficiency can be improved. This school of thought supports the use of techniques such as **cost accounting** and **work-study**.

One of the best-known members of the school of scientific management is **F. W. Taylor** (1856–1915). Taylor was a highly successful engineer who began to advise and lecture on management practices and became a consultant to Henry Ford. His theories were based on a simple interpretation of human behaviour, but some of his methods have survived across the years.

Taylor's ideas were formulated during his time at the Bethlehem Steel Company in the USA. He believed in firm management based on scientific principles, reflecting his background as an engineer. He used a stopwatch to measure how long various activities took and sought the most efficient methods of completing tasks. He then detailed 'normal' times in which duties should be completed, and assessed individual performance against these. Efficiency, he argued, would improve productivity, competitiveness and profits. This required employees to be organised, closely supervised and paid **piece rate** (according to how much they produced).

Taylor believed that people were 'economic animals' and solely motivated by money. Workers should have no control over their work and the social aspect of employment was considered irrelevant and ignored.

Taylor's views were unpopular with shop-floor employees and resulted in many strikes. As workers and managers became more highly educated, they sought other ways of motivating and organising employees.

Examiner's tip

You should see the theories of motivation as a whole and be familiar with their development over the twentieth century. This will aid you in assessing any given situation. But don't think that there is necessarily a 'right' answer. The success of a particular motivation technique will depend on the circumstances and the people involved.

The human relations school of management

A weakness of the scientific school was that its work ignored the social needs of employees. This, and the obvious unpopularity of the ideas of Taylor and other scientific managers such as Henri Fayol, led to the development of the human relations school. This school of thought concentrated on the sociological aspects of work.

The foremost member of the human relations school of management was an American psychologist, **Elton Mayo**. He is best remembered for his Hawthorne Studies at the Western Electric Company in Chicago between 1927 and 1932. He conducted experiments to discover whether employee performance was affected by factors such as breaks and the level of lighting. The results surprised Mayo. The productivity of one group of female employees increased both when the lighting was lessened and when it was increased. It became apparent that they were responding to the level of attention they were receiving as part of the investigations and because they were working together as a group. From this experiment, Mayo concluded that motivation depends on:

- the type of job being carried out and the type of supervision given to the employee
- group relationships, group morale and individuals' sense of worth

Mayo's work took forward the debate on management in general and motivation in particular. He moved the focus on to the needs of employees, rather than just the needs of the organisation. His legacy is seen in many companies, such as Honda, which make extensive use of team work and clearly believe that employees working together can improve the performance of all. Although Mayo's research is over 70 years old, it still has great relevance to businesses in the twenty-first century.

The neo-human relations school

Abraham Maslow and **Frederick Herzberg** are recognised as key members of this school of thought. They began to expound their views in the 1950s. While the human relations school associated with Elton Mayo highlighted the *sociological* aspects of work, the neo-human relations school considered the *psychological* aspects of employment.

Abraham Maslow

Abraham Maslow was an American psychologist who formulated a famous **hierarchy of needs** (Figure 5.6). According to Maslow, human needs consist of five types that form a hierarchy:

(1) Physiological — the need for food, shelter, water and sex.

(2) Security — the need to be free from threats and danger.

(3) Social — the need to love and be loved, and to be part of a group.

(4) Esteem — the need to have self-respect and the respect of colleagues.

(5) Self-actualisation — the need to develop personal skills and fulfil one's potential.

Maslow argued that all individuals have a hierarchy of needs and that once one level of needs is satisfied, people can be motivated by tasks that offer the opportunity to satisfy the next level of needs. In other words, once a safe working environment and a permanent contract have met an individual's security needs, other measures, such as working as part of a team, are necessary to motivate the employee.

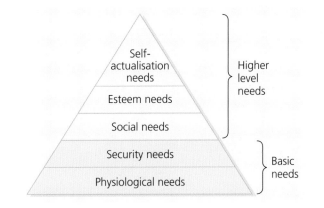

Figure 5.6 Maslow's hierarchy of needs

Some writers have cast doubt on the existence of a hierarchy of needs. They have argued that social needs and esteem needs may coexist and that people do not move smoothly up a hierarchy, as Maslow's model suggests. However, his work brings psychology into motivational theory and highlights the range of individual needs that may be met through employment.

Frederick Herzberg

The research carried out by Frederick Herzberg offered some support for Maslow's views and focused on the psychological aspects of motivation. Herzberg asked 203 accountants and engineers to identify those factors about their employment that pleased and displeased them. Figure 5.7 summarises Herzberg's findings.

This research was the basis of Herzberg's two-factor theory, first published in 1968. Herzberg divided the factors motivating people at work into two groups:

- **Motivators.** These are positive factors that give people job satisfaction (e.g. receiving recognition for effort) and therefore increase productivity as motivation rises.
- **Hygiene (or maintenance) factors.** These are factors that may cause dissatisfaction among employees. Herzberg argued that motivators should be built into the hygiene factors. Improving hygiene factors will not positively motivate but will reduce employee dissatisfaction. Examples of hygiene factors are pay, fair treatment and reasonable working conditions.

Herzberg did not argue that hygiene factors are unimportant. On the contrary, he contended that only when such factors are properly met can motivators begin to operate positively.

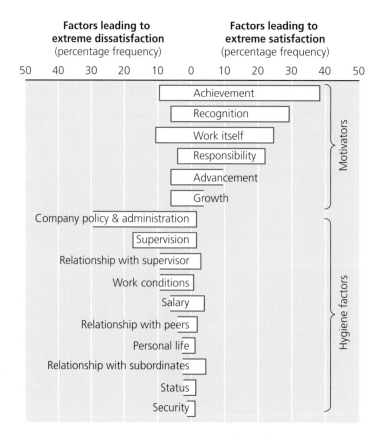

Figure 5.7 Herzberg's factors causing satisfaction and dissatisfaction

Process theories of motivation

The foremost writer on process theory is **Victor Vroom**, who published *Work and Motivation* in 1964. Vroom's theory expressed the view that motivation depends on people's expectations of the outcome. If working life offers opportunities for workers' expectations to be met, motivation is likely to be high. If the outcome of their actions is expected to be desirable, they will be motivated. The stronger the desire for the outcome, the greater is the level of motivation.

4.2 The use of financial methods to motivate employees

Some writers, such as Herzberg, believe that money is not a positive motivator, although the lack of it can demotivate. However, pay systems are nevertheless designed to motivate employees through money.

Piece-rate pay

Piece-rate pay gives a payment for each item produced. This system encourages effort, but often at the expense of quality. Piece rate is common in agriculture and the textile industry but is difficult to apply in service industries.

Commission

Commission is a payment made to employees based on the value of sales achieved. It can form all or part of a salary package.

Profit-related pay

Profit-related pay gives employees a share of the profits earned by the business. This is an approach adopted by the John Lewis Partnership. It encourages all employees to work hard to generate the maximum profits for the business. It also offers firms some flexibility: for example, in less prosperous times, wages can fall along with profits, so reducing the need for redundancies.

Performance-related pay

Performance-related pay is a topical but controversial technique used in many industries from textiles to education. It needs to be tied into some assessment or appraisal of employee performance. Whatever criteria are used to decide who should receive higher pay, the effect can be divisive and damaging to employee morale.

Share ownership

Employees are sometimes offered shares in the company in which they work. ASDA operates such a scheme. Shares can be purchased through savings schemes: for example, by shop-floor employees putting aside a few pounds each week. However, share ownership may cause discontentment if this perk is available only to the senior staff.

Share options

Some businesses offer senior managers and some other employees share options. These are the opportunity to purchase shares in the company at some future date and an agreed price. The employee will take up this option only if the share price is higher than the agreed price when the date arrives. It is hoped that employees will work hard to improve the business's performance (and its share price). If this happens, employees may be able to sell their shares and make an immediate profit.

4.3 Improving job design

Many theorists have argued that jobs need to be designed or redesigned with the major motivational factors in mind. They should not be too highly specialised and should offer a varied range of duties. Equally, jobs need to allow people to use their initiative as well as to meet their social needs by working with others.

Managers responding to the views of such theorists have realised that money may not be a great motivator and that financial incentive schemes can be difficult to operate. Working in teams may also mean that individual financial incentive schemes are of little relevance. A number of non-financial methods of motivation have therefore been developed.

Job enlargement

This technique gives employees a broader workload of a similar nature. This widens the variety of tasks that are completed and, hopefully, lessens the repetition and monotony that are all too common on production lines that rely on the division of labour. Job enlargement may offer advantages in the short term. This technique is also called **horizontal loading**.

Job rotation

Job rotation is similar to job enlargement. It widens the activities of a worker by switching him or her around a range of work. For example, it may require an employee in an office to move regularly between staffing reception and inputting data on to a database. Job rotation may offer the advantage of making it easier to cover for absent colleagues, but it may also reduce productivity as workers are initially unfamiliar with a new task.

Job enrichment

Job enrichment attempts to give employees greater responsibility by increasing the range and complexity of tasks they are called on to complete and giving them the necessary authority. It motivates by giving employees the opportunity to use their abilities to the fullest. Herzberg argued that job enrichment (through motivators) should be a central element in any policy of motivation. According to Herzberg, enriched jobs should contain a range of tasks and challenges at different ability levels, and clear opportunities for achievement and feedback on performance. Job enrichment necessitates training.

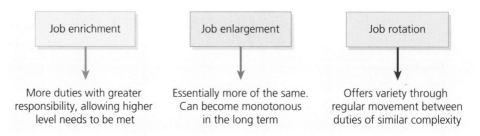

Figure 5.8 Job enrichment, enlargement and rotation

Developing and retaining an effective workforce: motivating employees

4.4 Team working and empowerment

Empowerment

Empowerment involves giving people control over their working lives. This can be achieved by organising the labour force into teams with a high degree of autonomy — this approach to management derives from the original work conducted by Mayo. Using such an approach means that employees plan their own work, take their own decisions and solve their own problems. Teams are set targets to achieve and may receive rewards for doing so. Empowered teams motivate through allowing people the opportunity to meet some of the higher needs identified by Maslow or Herzberg's motivators. Car manufacturers Volvo and Vauxhall use this technique to improve employee performance.

Examiner's tip

This is a common topic for examination questions, as empowered teams are a popular method of organising labour forces. It is important to appreciate the advantages and disadvantages of this approach. The advantages centre on the positive motivational effects. This can result in higher productivity, leading to improved competitiveness and higher profits or market share. Disadvantages (which may only exist in the short term) centre on the cost and disruption of training, and opposition from employees.

Quality circles

Quality circles are small groups of fewer than 20 people who meet regularly to discuss and solve production problems. They are in widespread use to allow employees an opportunity to contribute to decision making. The members are usually drawn from all levels and areas within the organisation. This ensures that all perspectives are considered. As well as motivating staff, such a group can provide businesses with some valuable ideas. This technique was first used at the Toyota Motor Company in Japan in the 1950s. It has been increasingly adopted in the West since the 1980s.

Single status

Single status occurs where a business has removed all the barriers that distinguish between various grades of staff. These forms of distinction may include:
- canteens and other social facilities
- different pay systems (salaries versus piece-rate)
- different clothing (managers wearing suits and shop-floor workers wearing overalls)

Removing these barriers is intended to eliminate the 'them and us' attitude that is common in business. The concept of single status originated in Japan but now operates worldwide.

CHAPTER 6 Operations management

1 Making operational decisions

What you need to know:
- operational targets
- calculating and managing capacity utilisation
- operational issues dealing with non-standard orders and matching supply and demand

1.1 Operational targets

Business may have three different types of operational target:
- unit costs
- quality targets
- capacity utilisation targets

Unit costs

Unit costs are the cost of producing a single, average unit of output. This may be either a good or a service. Unit costs are calculated by using this formula:

$$\text{unit costs} = \frac{\text{total costs}}{\text{units of output}}$$

For example, if a passenger ferry has 120 passengers and the total cost of a single journey is £2,400, the unit cost of carrying a single passenger is £20. This is the ferry business's unit cost. Businesses will seek to reduce their unit costs, subject to meeting customers' needs in terms of quality.

Quality targets

Quality is meeting the needs of a customer. Businesses may set quality targets in terms of:
- only having a certain (low) percentage of faulty products, or possibly no faults — known as 'zero defects'
- reducing the number of customer complaints to a specified level
- achieving certain targets for customer satisfaction (as measured through market research)

Capacity utilisation

Capacity utilisation measures the extent to which a business uses the production resources that are available to it. The passenger ferry mentioned above may be able to carry 200 people on a single journey, but if it only carries 100 passengers, it is only using 50% of its resources. By increasing capacity utilisation, a business may be able to increase its revenue with only a relatively small increase in costs. We consider capacity utilisation more fully below.

1.2 Calculating and managing capacity utilisation

What is capacity?

A firm's **capacity** is the maximum amount that the firm is physically capable of producing if it uses its available resources to their fullest extent. Over time, a firm is likely to adjust its capacity to meet the demands of the marketplace. The following factors may affect the amount of capacity a business requires:

● the entry (or departure) of a competitor to (or from) the market
● a change in tastes or fashions, meaning higher or lower demand for the product
● new developments in products or new production techniques

A firm may adjust capacity by:
● investing in a completely new factory, shop or office
● extending an existing facility
● closing down premises permanently
● closing down premises temporarily ('mothballing')

Examiner's tip

To be able to write analytically in this area, as in many others, you should appreciate the circumstances in which each of the above techniques might be employed. For example, a firm facing a short-term decline in the sales of its products may mothball a factory during a slump.

What is capacity utilisation?

Capacity utilisation measures the amount or proportion of a business's currently available capacity that is being used in production. Changes in demand and competitors' actions will affect the extent of capacity utilisation.

$$\text{capacity utilisation (\%)} = \frac{\text{current output per month}}{\text{maximum output per month}} \times 100$$

Managing capacity utilisation

If a business under-utilises its capacity, it is said to have **spare capacity**. There are a number of consequences, most of which are unfavourable:
● The business is likely to face higher unit costs, as fixed overheads are spread over fewer units of output.
● This will adversely affect profits or competitiveness, since the firm is likely to charge higher prices as a consequence of excess capacity.
● Labour and other resources may be idle, which can have a negative effect on levels of motivation.
● The firm might produce more output than it can sell, leading to increased storage costs and the possibility of being forced to sell products at a discount later.
● It may be necessary to lay off staff, adversely affecting the corporate image of the business.

Because of these factors, businesses are keen to implement strategies to avoid having spare or unutilised capacity. There are two broad options open to the firm:
● **Increase sales to use up the available capacity.** Entering new markets might achieve this — perhaps overseas, or by finding new uses for an existing product. Kellogg's increased sales of its cornflakes by promoting them as a product to be consumed at any time of the day, not solely at breakfast.
● **Reduce the capacity available to the firm.** This is known as **rationalisation**. It may mean selling land and buildings, as well as other fixed assets, and making staff redundant. This can be a very unattractive and expensive option, and firms may lease out spare capacity, transferring employees to other jobs if possible.

A business might face circumstances in which it has insufficient capacity and cannot meet demand for its products. In such a situation it has two options:

- Increase capacity by purchasing more fixed assets (factories, machinery). This is likely to be expensive and take time to put into practice.
- Subcontract production by finding a supplier to manufacture or supply part or all of the good or service. This is cheaper than increasing capacity and may be put into operation in the short term.

The decision depends upon whether the firm believes that the increase in demand will last. If so, it is more likely to increase its productive capacity permanently.

1.3 Operational issues dealing with non-standard orders and matching supply and demand

Non-standard orders

Non-standard orders occur when a customer asks a supplier for products that do not meet the normal specifications for that supplier. For example, a supplier of tinned lentils might normally supply 400 gram cans in boxes of 24. However, an order from a supermarket might request a smaller can size (say 300 grams) in boxes of 18 because they are easier to put on display in its shops.

Meeting this order would involve a number of operational issues for the supplier of lentils:

- The business will require a different range of cans and boxes to meet the requirements of the order.
- The business's processing and packaging equipment will need to be adjusted before and after supplying this order.
- These changes are likely to lead to delays on the production line.
- The operational costs of supplying this order are likely to be greater.

Should the business accept the order? The answer depends on how important this customer is. A large supermarket might place many large-scale orders for lentils and other products, and therefore be a very important customer. In this case, the firm might accept the order and also any consequent drop in profits. For a less important customer this might not be the case. A business that is seeking to expand may also accept the order as a means of increasing sales and market share, so long as it does not damage its overall profits.

Non-standard orders can take a number of different forms, such as the following:

- The owner of holiday homes in the Lake District might receive requests to book three cottages for a 5-night period rather than the usual week.
- A restaurant might be asked by a business to open during the afternoon to host a special business function.
- A supplier of olive oil might be asked to provide some of the product flavoured with lemon, which is not a part of its normal range of products.

- A car hire company may be asked by a customer to supply a car for one-way travel, borrowing the car in one town and leaving it in another.

Matching supply and demand

This is a problem for businesses that face seasonal patterns of demand. Businesses such as fruit farms, holiday camps and some hotels face difficulties in matching the amount they supply with the volume that customers wish to purchase. In many ways, this is a matter of managing capacity, as discussed earlier in this chapter. Managers can aim to increase capacity at certain times of the year, or possibly seek alternative uses for spare capacity when demand is low.

2 *Developing effective operations: quality*

What you need to know:
- the meaning of quality
- the distinction between quality control and quality assurance
- systems of quality assurance
- quality standards

2.1 The meaning of quality

A quality product is one that meets customers' needs fully. Quality is a major determinant of a business's competitiveness and has attracted a great deal of attention over recent years. A quality product does not need to be a costly or premium product.

If a firm produces poor quality products, it incurs:
- the costs of scrapping or reworking products
- additional costs if customers return goods for repair under warranty
- costs (which are more difficult to measure) associated with damage to the reputation of the business

Quality can be important to businesses for the following reasons:
- It can provide a business with a unique selling point (USP), helping small businesses to compete against larger rivals.
- It can allow businesses to charge higher prices, increasing their profit margins.
- Supplying a high quality product can enable a business to achieve higher sales.

2.2 The distinction between quality control and quality assurance

Quality control

There is an important distinction between quality control and quality assurance. **Quality control** is the process of checking that completed production meets agreed criteria. Quality control inspectors usually undertake this task, though some factories encourage employees to check their own quality. However, quality control only identifies problems once the production process is complete. Quality control also aims to improve product design and entails the regular review of quality control procedures.

Quality assurance

Quality assurance is implemented to ensure that quality standards are attained by all employees in a business. The aim is to maximise customer satisfaction and hence sales and profits. This policy affects all activities in the organisation and is intended to prevent problems, such as defective products, from occurring in the first place.

2.3 Systems of quality assurance

There are a number of different systems of quality assurance, of which **total quality management** (TQM) is probably the best known. TQM instils a culture of quality throughout the organisation. It places on all employees of a firm an individual and collective responsibility for maintaining high quality standards. It aims for prevention rather than detection, with a target of zero defects (see Figure 6.1).

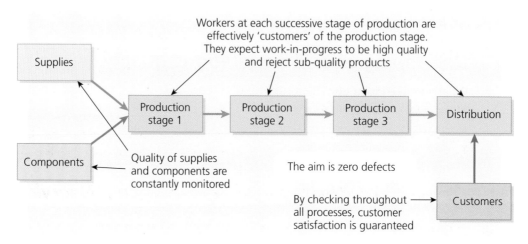

Figure 6.1 Total quality management

TQM originated in Japan and was based on the work of an American consultant, Edward Deming. In the 1950s and 1960s, Japanese products were regarded as relatively cheap but inferior versions of products manufactured in Western economies. In response to this, Japanese companies began to develop the philosophies and systems necessary to acquire a reputation for quality products.

TQM has both an internal and an external dimension. Externally, the success of a firm depends on its ability to satisfy the demands of its external customers. Product quality is likely to be a way in which a company can achieve a competitive advantage. Internally, each department in a firm is viewed as a customer and/or a supplier. The firm has to meet high standards in this 'internal' trading — the flow of raw materials, components and finished goods through to the dispatch department.

Quality assurance systems are unlikely to succeed without the support of the whole workforce. Workers must understand and comply with them. TQM seeks to establish a unity of interest and commitment to the maintenance of the highest possible quality standards in each of the internal transactions. It seeks to minimise the amount of time and money spent on quality control by preventing quality problems. Individual commitment to quality can be reinforced by the operation of quality circles (see page 69) and other employee participation schemes.

TQM ensures that products are constantly monitored throughout manufacture. Workers at each stage of the process examine critically the work-in-progress they receive. Errors and faults are identified and rectified at the earliest possible stage, and customer satisfaction is assured.

2.4 Quality standards

A **quality standard** is awarded to businesses that have put into place certain systems that enable certain quality targets to be met.

ISO 9000 is the standard most commonly available to businesses in the European Union (EU). The UK equivalent of this standard is BS 5750. Businesses have to meet criteria to receive certification that shows this standard is being met. They have to establish and maintain an effective quality system to demonstrate that products or services conform to it.

BSI and ISO systems are based on documentary evidence that specified procedures and processes are followed. Hence, they can become very bureaucratic. As a result, critics have said that this quality system says more about firms' adherence to procedures than about the actual quality of their products or services.

In spite of this criticism, ISO 9000 remains an important international indicator of quality and some firms will not trade with businesses that are not certified.

3 *Developing effective operations: customer service*

What you need to know:
- what is customer service?
- methods of meeting customer expectations
- monitoring and improving customer service
- the benefits of high levels of customer service

3.1 What is customer service?

Customer service is a range of activities designed to improve the degree of satisfaction experienced by a business's customers. One objective of customer service is to meet or exceed a customer's expectations from using the good or service.

Customer service can take a number of forms, including the following:
- **Personal assistance.** Offering customers advice and support while they are looking for a product or using a service is a common technique. For example, supermarkets often offer to pack shopping bags for customers or carry heavy items to the car.
- **Online customer service.** Many firms offer customer service via the internet. For example, customers can purchase products 24 hours a day, 365 days every year. This approach allows customers to shop without leaving home or incurring travel costs. This type of customer service involves a degree of self-service.

3.2 Methods of meeting customer service expectations

There are a number of methods of meeting a customer's expectations:
- **Finding out what customers expect.** By understanding what a customer expects from a good or service, a business is able to ensure that it provides whatever is necessary to meet the customer's expectations. This is likely to involve the use of primary market research to ensure that the precise expectations of this group of customers are identified.

- **Recruiting the right employees and providing training.** This is important for all businesses, but arguably more so for those providing a service where there is greater contact between employees and customers. Employees should receive the necessary training to enable them to meet customers' expectations as fully as possible. In addition, training may be given to enable employees to gather information about any changes in the needs of customers over time. This can help a business to be flexible in a market where tastes and fashions may change.

Figure 6.2 Key issues in customer service

- **Communicating effectively.** Customers' expectations are more likely to be met by a business that communicates well with its customers. This may involve providing clear information on products or services as well as information on prices and who to ask for further information. Employees should have sufficient training to enable them to answer customers' questions efficiently. It is also important for senior employees to make sure they communicate their understanding of customer expectations to all employees within the business.
- **Taking a long-term view of customer relationships.** Some customers may ask for special requirements, such as quick delivery, which may entail extra expense in the short term. However, this could offer great benefits in the long term in the form of customer loyalty and positive publicity via word-of-mouth.
- **Implementing a quality system.** Quality control systems are designed to remove faulty products from the production system before they reach the customer. This approach to quality can be effective in helping to meet customer expectations, but it does assume that substandard products will be allowed to pass through the production system. Alternatively, a business might use a system of quality assurance, such as TQM, which aims to avoid any quality errors.

Examiner's tip

Think about how different businesses will meet their customers' expectations. This will help you to apply your knowledge on customer service. How might a family butcher meet customer expectations? Contrast this with the way in which a garden design company might do the same thing.

- **Quality standards.** Quality standards such as ISO 9000 ensure that firms use systems designed to meet quality targets time and time again. Possession of these standards also shows that businesses have systems in place to rectify any failures to meet quality targets. Quality standards can be an important element of meeting customers' expectations on a regular basis.

3.3 Monitoring and improving customer service

It is important that managers do not become complacent about their customer service provision. Even those businesses that provide excellent customer service may find that their position is eroded as standards are allowed to slip or as competitors introduce new and improved standards. For example, some businesses may find that rival businesses have improved their offerings by opening for longer hours or offering improved after-sales service. It is important to recognise that consumer expectations can rise over time.

A business can monitor the level of its customer service by using a range of techniques to survey its customers and to compare expectations and experiences. This might be done by:
- asking customers to complete online surveys
- telephoning customers who have recently bought a good or service to enquire about their experiences
- leaving monitoring cards for customers to complete — this is common in hotels
- employing market research agencies to carry out monitoring work with a sample of customers

The techniques that a business deploys to monitor the quality of its customer service and the degree to which its customers' expectations are met will depend on the finance it has available to it.

Examiner's tip

A well-managed business will investigate weaknesses in its customer service provision before taking decisions on how to improve it. The actual approach taken will depend on the results of this research, the nature of the business and the market in which it trades.

Methods of improving customer service are shown in section 3.2. They usually involve expenditure on training, high-quality recruitment, market research and implementing (or improving) quality systems.

3.4 The benefits of high levels of customer service

A business that offers high levels of customer service will receive a range of possible benefits, including those set out below.
- **The ability to charge premium prices.** Businesses that are recognised as meeting customers' expectations may be able to charge higher prices because demand is relatively price inelastic. In these circumstances, customers are more likely to remain loyal to a business even when its prices rise.
- **The ability to use customer service as a unique selling point (USP).** A reputation for high-quality customer service can enable a business to differentiate its products from those offered by rival businesses. This can be used as a basis for promoting a product. You can find out more about unique selling points on page 82.

● **The maintenance of customer loyalty.** Customers may be more likely to continue to purchase the goods or services of a particular business if they feel that their expectations are met. This can have positive effects on sales revenues and profits.

4 Developing effective operations: working with suppliers

What you need to know:
● choosing effective suppliers
● how suppliers can help a business to improve its operational performance

4.1 Choosing effective suppliers

Suppliers provide businesses with products and services that are essential for the organisation to carry out its commercial activities. A supplier may provide a business with one or more of the following:
● raw materials and fuel
● components such as electrical systems and tyres for car manufacturers
● services such as support on environmental protection or health and safety
● capital assets, such as buildings and machinery, which may only be purchased infrequently

A supplier will be considered effective if it meets a number of criteria:
● **Reliability and flexibility.** An effective supplier will always deliver on time and to the agreed specification. It will also be flexible and able to meet a sudden change in requirements (in terms of either volume or specification) on the part of its customer.
● **Ability to offer competitive prices.** An effective supplier will be able to deliver supplies within the customer's price range as a result of operating efficiently itself. This is important if its customers are to maintain their profit margins and to avoid adverse budget variances. An effective supplier will also be able to control its own costs, especially during a period when inflation is rising, as is happening in the UK at the time of writing.
● **Ability to meet the customer's specifications.** A manufacturer of organic foods will require organic ingredients. The owners of a large sports stadium will require trained security staff. If a supplier is to be effective, it must be able to meet the precise needs of its customers. If it fails to do so, the business buying from the supplier may, in turn, not be able to meet the expectations of its customers, thereby damaging its reputation and sales figures.
● **Payment terms.** Cash flow is an important factor for many small and medium-sized businesses. If a supplier can offer trade credit, this makes it very attractive to businesses as it delays cash outflows and can improve the business's cash position. It is not unusual for suppliers to offer 30 or 60 days' trade credit (i.e. time to pay) in order to win customers.

A supplier is more likely to be judged effective if it continues to have a relationship with the business over the long term. Thus, many businesses look to establish partnerships with suppliers. This happens when suppliers meet the conditions set out above, and in return the customers pay on the agreed date, offer fair prices and communicate regularly with the supplier to advise them of any changes in their requirements well in advance.

4.2 How suppliers can help a business to improve its operational performance

An effective supplier offers a number of benefits to its customers:

- **Enabling the customer business to operate within agreed budgets.** If it delivers its products at the agreed price, the customer business should not suffer an adverse variance on its budgets.
- **Assisting the customer business in meeting the expectations of its own customers.** It does this by always delivering the required quantity on time and to the agreed specification.
- **Offering support and advice on the supplies it provides.** For example, a business supplying a technical component might provide advice on relevant technological developments.
- **Responding quickly to changes in the size of its orders.** This enables the customer business to meet seasonal demand or sudden rush orders.
- **Helping the business to operate its quality systems and meet its targets.** It does this through the reliability of its service and its ability to meet the order specification.

5 *Using technology in operations*

What you need to know:

- types of technology used in operations
- issues in introducing and updating technology

5.1 Types of technology used in operations

Technology is advancing at an ever-increasing rate and affects the way in which businesses produce goods and services as well as the products themselves. Technological developments that may affect production include:

- more advanced and sophisticated computer systems, allowing, for example, automated stock control systems and electronic data interchange
- the internet, which enhances a business's ability to market and sell its products as well as its ability to communicate with its customers
- computer-aided manufacture (CAM), where manufacturers use robots as an integral part of the production process
- computer-aided design (CAD), which can be linked to CAM systems

As this list shows, technological advances have created new ways of making and selling products. For example, changes in technology mean that even small businesses can benefit from developments in stock control and design technology. This assists them to improve the quality of their product or service, and therefore to compete with larger-scale competitors.

Developments in technology have dramatically improved the process of production for many firms — services as well as manufacturing. The development of computer-aided design (CAD) has made the design of new products easier to carry out, store and alter. Modern software can also be used to estimate the cost of newly designed products. Technology has revolutionised manufacturing too. Computer-aided manufacturing is used by manufacturing firms of all sizes. Computers control the machines on the production line, saving labour and costs, and CAM systems can be linked to CAD technology to transform the entire process.

5.2 Issues in introducing and updating technology

Benefits of new and updated technology

New technology offers businesses and consumers a range of benefits:

- It reduces unit costs of production, enhancing the competitiveness of the business concerned. For example, design technology allows even relatively small publishers to send books electronically to be printed overseas, where labour and other costs are lower.
- In the case of high-technology products, such as new games consoles, it offers the opportunity to charge a premium price until the competition catches up. Such price skimming is likely to boost profits.
- Technology offers the chance to improve quality by, for example, ensuring a consistent standard of quality through the use of CAM.
- Small to medium-sized businesses may benefit from technology in terms of improved productivity. Using technology efficiently may enable employees to work more efficiently. For example, EPOS (electronic point of sale) systems record information on sales and prices, and can be operated by the checkout operator in a shop as an ordinary part of his or her work. This automatically adjusts stock levels and can reorder stock automatically as well as providing data to calculate sales revenue figures.
- It may allow access to new markets: for example, the internet allows online bookshops to sell worldwide.
- The use of technology can reduce waste. Modern water control systems in commercial buildings recycle rainwater and other water for reuse within the business.

Costs of new and updated technology

New technology also poses difficulties for many businesses. For example:

- It is likely to be a drain on an organisation's capital. In some circumstances, firms may experience difficulty in raising the funds necessary to install high-technology equipment or to research a new product.
- It almost inevitably requires training of the existing workforce and perhaps recruitment of new employees. Both actions can create considerable costs for businesses.
- Its introduction may be met with opposition from existing employees, especially if job security is threatened. This may lead to industrial relations problems.

CHAPTER 7 Marketing and the competitive environment

1 Effective marketing

What you need to know:
- the nature and purpose of marketing
- the benefits and drawbacks of niche and mass marketing
- what is the marketing mix?

1.1 The nature and purpose of marketing

What is marketing and what is its purpose in business?

A number of definitions of marketing exist. According to the Chartered Institute of Marketing, **marketing** is defined as:

> 'the management process which identifies, anticipates and supplies customer requirements efficiently and profitably'

A wider definition is:

> 'Marketing is the human activity directed at satisfying needs and wants through the exchange process.'

Marketing involves a wide range of activities in businesses, including:
- research
- advertising
- design
- promotion
- testing
- distribution
- quality control and assurance
- packaging
- pricing
- after-sales service

Following the lead of Japanese businesses, many companies have disbanded their marketing departments, recognising that marketing affects everyone in the firm, from receptionists and shop-floor workers, to engineers, managers and directors.

Marketing has a number of functions in a business. It collects and analyses data on markets and consumer behaviour. Once analysed, this information can be used to guide businesses as to the products they should produce and the best methods to promote them. It encourages planning and target setting and the use of a more scientific approach to management and decision making. Furthermore, it encourages a business to be outward looking: to assess the actions and activities of rivals, pressure groups, governments and consumers, for example.

Some would argue that marketing should be the guiding philosophy for all the activities of a business. According to Peter Drucker, 'there is only one valid definition of business purpose: to create a customer'.

The distinction between consumer marketing and business-to-business marketing

Consumer marketing encompasses those activities involved in selling a product to an individual who is the end user, that is, the person who consumes the product. This is also described as business-to-consumer marketing or B2C marketing.

In contrast, **business-to-business marketing** (B2B marketing) describes the range of activities undertaken by one business when marketing its products to another business. For example, a supplier of gas ovens may advertise in a trade magazine read by the owners of restaurants and hotels in the hope of selling to some of these businesses.

1.2 The benefits and drawbacks of niche and mass marketing

Niche marketing occurs when businesses identify and satisfy the demands of small segments of a larger market. Well-known examples of businesses engaging in niche marketing are Tie Rack and the radio station Classic FM. Classic FM serves the niche of radio listeners who wish to listen to popular classical music.

The advantages and disadvantages of niche marketing are as follows:
- The first company to identify a niche market can often gain a dominant market position as consumers become loyal to the product — even if its price is higher.
- Niche markets can be highly profitable, as companies operating in them often have the opportunity to charge premium prices.
- Because sales may be relatively low, firms operating in niche markets may not be able to spread fixed overheads over sufficient sales to attain acceptable profit margins.
- If a niche market proves to be profitable, it is likely to attract new competition, making it less attractive to the companies that first discovered the market.

Mass marketing occurs when businesses aim their products at most of the available market. Many small and medium-sized businesses sell in mass markets. One example is Working Title Films — a company that makes films, a number of which have proved popular with mass market audiences. The company's best-known film is probably *Four Weddings and a Funeral*.

Examiner's tip

This is a common topic for examination questions. Examiners frequently ask whether a move into a niche market, or from a niche to a mass market, is a wise strategy. You should consider the type of market and the type of firm in developing your answer, and make sure you apply your response to the scenario throughout.

Businesses must be able to produce on a large scale if they are to sell successfully in a mass market. This may mean that the firm has to invest heavily in resources such as buildings, machinery and vehicles. Often firms have to be price competitive to flourish in mass markets, or to have a unique selling point (USP) that makes the company and its products distinctive. However, firms supplying mass markets frequently produce large numbers of similar, standardised products, making production easier. They can also benefit from **economies of scale**, reducing the costs of producing a single unit of production and thereby enhancing profit margins.

1.3 What is the marketing mix?

The **marketing mix** refers to the main variables comprising a firm's marketing strategy. The four main elements of the mix are:
- **product** — including design, features and functions
- **price** — pricing strategies and tactics
- **promotion** — a range of activities including advertising, public relations (PR) and branding
- **place** — distribution channels and retail outlets

These elements are sometimes referred to as the **four Ps**. Some writers identify more than four Ps, including factors such as **packaging** and **people**.

2 Using the marketing mix: product

What you need to know:
- the influences on the development of new goods and services
- the importance of unique selling points (USPs)
- product portfolio analysis, including the Boston matrix and the product life cycle

2.1 The influences on the development of new goods and services

A number of factors have an effect upon the development of new goods and services:
- **Technology.** Developments in technology are at the heart of many of the new products that come on to the market. Advances in battery life have helped to generate a range of more efficient electric cars and smaller and lighter mobile phones and laptop computers. Similarly, developments in biotechnology have resulted in the creation of plants with resistance to particular adverse climatic conditions. Firms use these technological advances as the basis for the development of new products that meet the needs of consumers more fully.
- **Competitors' actions.** A competitor producing a new product can be a spur to a rival to produce something that is at least as good, if not better. Businesses that own hotels have attempted to improve their services in a variety of ways: for example, by offering guests a choice of different types of pillow in an attempt to provide a more restful night.
- **The entrepreneurial skills of managers and owners.** One of the talents of successful entrepreneurs is creativity. The skill of being able to think up new ideas for goods and services that fit with customer needs leads to the development of many new products. In 2006 Pauline Clifford established a successful business called Starsparkles. Her product idea was to decorate customers' shoes with a range of coloured, sparkly patterns. The business has been very successful.

Examiner's tip

You will be better prepared for likely questions on this area if you try to think about the factors that influence the development of new products by small and medium-sized businesses.

2.2 The importance of unique selling points

Businesses commonly add value by creating a **unique selling point** or **proposition** (USP) for their products. A USP allows a business to differentiate its products from others in the market. This can help the business in a number of ways:

- The business can base its advertising campaigns around the (real or perceived) difference between its product and those of its rivals.
- Having a USP assists in encouraging brand loyalty, as its gives customers a reason to continue to buy that particular business's product.
- A USP commonly allows the firm to charge a premium price for the product.

For example, British Bakeries differentiates its Hovis-branded 'Best of Both' bread as looking and tasting like white bread, while possessing the nutritional advantages of brown bread.

2.3 Product portfolio analysis including the product life cycle and the Boston matrix

The product life cycle

The **product life cycle** is the theory that all products follow a similar pattern throughout their life. The five stages are: development, introduction, growth, maturity and decline. Products take varying amounts of time to pass through these stages. The Mars bar was launched in the 1920s and is still going strong. In contrast, the entire sales life span of Virtual Pets was about 2 years, while modern motor cars are expected to have a life cycle of about 10 years. The five stages are outlined below and illustrated in Figure 7.1.

(1) Development. Firms undertake research and development to create new products that will be their future best sellers. Many products fall by the wayside, as they do not meet the demands of consumers. This can be a very expensive stage, especially for firms operating in industries such as pharmaceuticals and electronic engineering. Cash flow is expected to be negative at this stage of a product's life.

(2) Introduction. This stage commences with the product's initial appearance on the market. At this time, sales are zero and the product has a negative cash flow. As time passes, sales should begin to rise, providing the company with some revenue. However, costs will remain high. The failure rate for new products is quite high, ranging from 60% to 90%, depending on the industry. When a product is ready to be launched, the seller must ensure that potential buyers are aware of the new product. This can be expensive and cash flow will remain negative. The price may have to be high to recoup the high initial costs of launching the product. For these reasons, many products never pass this stage.

(3) Growth. During the growth stage, sales rise rapidly and a firm's cash flow can improve considerably. The business's profits per unit sold are likely to be at a maximum. This is because firms tend to charge a high price at this stage, particularly if the product is innovatory. Firms with a technically superior good may well engage in **price skimming** (see page 91). The growth stage is critical to a product's survival. The product's success will depend on how competitors react to it. Profits per product can fall as more competitors enter the market and drive the price down, while creating the need for heavy promotional expenditure by the original firm. At this point, a typical marketing strategy encourages strong brand loyalty to fight off the new competition.

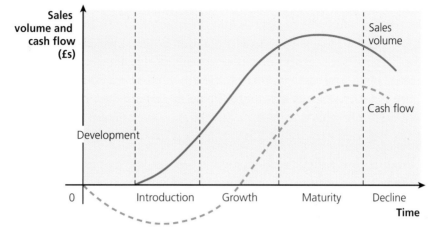

Figure 7.1 The product life cycle

(4) Maturity. During the maturity stage, the sales curve peaks and begins to decline. Both cash flow and profits also decline. This stage is characterised by severe competition with many brands in the market. Competitors emphasise improvements and differences in their versions of the product. Producers that remain in the market must make fresh promotional and distribution efforts. These efforts must focus on dealers as much as consumers to ensure that the product remains visible to the public. At this stage, consumers of the product know a lot about it and require specialist deals to attract their interest.

(5) Decline. During the decline stage, sales fall rapidly. New technology or a new product change may cause product sales to decline sharply. When this happens, marketing managers consider pruning items from the product line to eliminate those which are not earning a profit. At this stage, promotional efforts will be cut too.

Extension strategies

Firms may attempt to prolong the life of a product as it enters the decline stage by implementing **extension strategies**. They may use one or more of the following techniques:

- **Finding new markets for existing products.** Some companies selling baby milk have targeted less economically developed countries.
- **Encouraging people to use the product more frequently.** Breakfast cereals are often promoted as an evening snack.
- **Changing the appearance or packaging.** Some motor manufacturers have produced old models of cars with new colours or other features to extend the lives of their products.

Examiner's tip

For all major theories, such as the product life cycle, you should be able to give some assessment of the theory's strengths and weaknesses. This will help you to write evaluatively as well as confirming your understanding. An advantage of the life cycle might be that it helps a firm to plan (and finance) new products. Weaknesses might centre on the fact that different products are likely to have very different life cycles. A slump in sales might be due to external factors rather than the product entering its decline stage.

The product mix

The product life cycle highlights that, in spite of extension strategies, products have finite lives of varying length. A well-organised business will plan its product range so that it has products in each of the major stages of the life cycle: as one product reaches decline, replacements are entering the growth and maturity stages of their lives (see Figure 7.2). This means that there will be a constant flow of income from products in the mature phase of their lives to finance the development of new products.

Firms can achieve this goal in two ways:
- **Product line policy** — extending the product line by producing variants on existing products. For example, a small brewery might produce versions of its ales flavoured with chocolate or fruit.
- **Product mix policy** — developing new products. For example, the brewery above may introduce an entirely new beer, possibly a light summer ale.

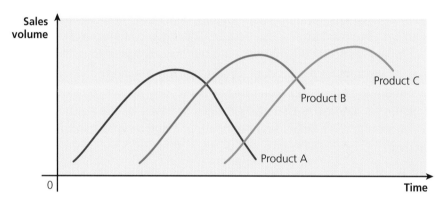

Figure 7.2 A healthy product mix

The Boston matrix

A number of tools are available to aid marketing managers in planning their product mix and strategy. One of the best known of these techniques is the Boston matrix produced by the Boston Consulting Group. The matrix allows businesses to undertake product portfolio analysis and is based on the premise that a product's market growth rate and its market share are important considerations in determining the marketing strategy.

The matrix, as shown in Figures 7.3 and 7.4, places products into four categories:
- **Star** products have a dominant share of the market and good prospects for growth.
- **Cash cows** are products with a dominant share of the market but low prospects for growth.
- **Dogs** have a low share of the market and no prospects for growth.
- **Problem children** are products that have a small share of a growing market and generally require a lot of funds to fulfil their potential.

A number of conclusions can be drawn from the Boston matrix:
- Firms should avoid having too many products in any single category. Obviously, firms do not want lots of dogs, but they also need to avoid having too many stars and problem children.
- Products in the top half of the chart are in the early stages of their life cycle and are in growing markets, but the cost of developing and promoting them will not have been recovered.

- Continuing production of cash cows will provide the necessary cash to develop the newer products. Cash cows will have passed the development stage, will have recovered their initial costs and will not require high promotional expenditure.
- Firms need problem child products as they may become tomorrow's cash cows.

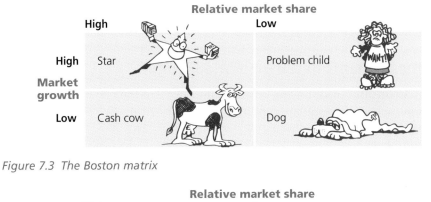

Figure 7.3 The Boston matrix

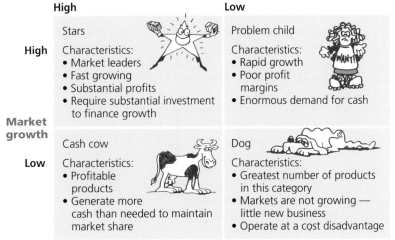

Figure 7.4 Features of the components of the marketing mix

Using the marketing mix: promotion

What you need to know:

- what is promotion?
- the elements of the marketing mix
- the influences on a business's choice of promotional mix

3.1 What is promotion?

Promotion is bringing consumers' attention to a product or business. Promotion aims to achieve targets including:

- to attract new customers and retain existing customers
- to improve the position of the business in the market
- to ensure the survival and growth of the business
- to increase awareness of a product
- to remind consumers about a product
- to show that a product is better than that of a competitor
- to improve the image of a product or company
- to support an existing product

3.2 The elements of the promotional mix

The **promotional mix** is the combination of methods used by businesses to communicate with prospective customers to inform them of their products and to persuade them to purchase these products. In effect, this is the promotion element of the marketing mix.

Figure 7.5 The promotional mix

Advertising

This is a paid form of non-personal communication using mass media such as television and newspapers. It aims to change the attitudes and buying behaviour of consumers. Expenditure on advertising has grown enormously over recent years. Advertising can be separated into two types:

● **Informative advertising.** This is designed to increase consumer awareness of a product. This type of advertising provides consumers with factual information. Such adverts centre on the prices and features of the products being advertised. Examples are classified adverts in newspapers.

● **Persuasive advertising.** This attempts to get consumers to purchase a particular product. Such advertising claims that the product in question is better than the competition. Some analysts contend that persuasive advertising distorts consumer spending by creating patterns of expenditure that might not occur naturally.

Sales promotions and merchandising

Merchandising is in-store promotional activity by manufacturers or retailers at the point of sale. Confectionery manufacturers such as Mars and Cadbury make extensive use of merchandising. Merchandising can be important when:

● consumers make purchasing decisions at the point of sale
● competitors make extensive use of merchandising

- a variety of rival products are on display in stores
- the products available have only minor differences

Other forms of sales promotion include:
- special offers
- competitions
- in-store demonstrations
- coupons, vouchers and free gifts
- reductions in price

These forms of promotion may be used when rival businesses wish to avoid initiating a price war, with all the uncertainties that this might entail. Depending on the circumstances, they can be relatively cheap, but they are often imprecise in targeting potential groups of consumers.

Packaging

Packaging assists in emphasising the attractiveness of the product and informing consumers of its features, functions and ingredients or contents as appropriate. Packaging has another important function: that of protecting the good during its distribution to ensure that it reaches the consumer in perfect condition. Some consumer groups have complained that products have too much packaging and many businesses are seeking to reduce the amount and to ensure that the materials used can be recycled.

Exhibitions and trade fairs

These are events staged to attract all those people involved in a particular market, both sellers and buyers. An example is the Good Food Show held in Birmingham each year, which attracts over 500 sellers of food and drink products and many potential customers.

Branding

This establishes an identity for a product that distinguishes it from the competition. Successful branding allows higher prices to be charged and can extend its life cycle by creating customer loyalty. Brand loyalty occurs when consumers regularly purchase particular products. Demand from such customers is unlikely to be price elastic, enabling the firm to increase the price level without much effect on demand. Brand loyalty can be active or passive. Active loyalty is a preference on the part of customers for a particular product. Passive loyalty is the result of consumer inertia — people get used to a purchasing pattern, which they do not change. Firms introducing new products can find this a major barrier to gaining a foothold in the market.

Personal selling

Personal selling involves visits by a firm's sales representatives to prospective customers. This may be used more in business-to-business selling, or in selling expensive products such as double glazing. It is usually achieved through the efforts of a team of sales representatives. Sales 'reps', as they are known, may sell to retailers or knock on the doors of potential customers. Personal selling is frequently used when the product is:
- highly technical (e.g. financial services) and requires explanation
- different from those produced by rivals and this requires emphasis
- expensive and consumers may require persuasion at a personal level before making a purchase

Personal selling is a relatively expensive method of raising public awareness of a product. It is frequently used as a method of promoting new products and collecting orders. It also provides a useful route for the collection of market research.

Public relations

Public relations (PR) is promoting the company's image to establish a favourable public attitude towards the company. Public relations aims to improve the image of a business and its products in the expectation of increasing sales. Firms can engage in a variety of public relations exercises, such as:

- making donations to charities or engaging in activities to benefit society, such as building children's playgrounds
- calling press conferences or issuing press releases to portray the company or its products in a positive light
- sponsoring sporting and cultural activities — funds obtained in this way are very important to, for example, the football Premier League and opera in the UK
- allowing visits to the company by members of the public and particularly school parties
- operating a high-profile customer relations department and responding promptly to any complaints

Public relations can be an expensive form of promotion for businesses and its impact on sales and profits is often difficult to determine. However, businesses with a national or international reputation are likely to feel the need to guard this precious asset. Public relations can be an effective way of achieving this.

3.4 Influences on the choice of promotional mix

Managers will take into account a range of factors when deciding on the precise promotional mix to be deployed:

- **The product's position in its life cycle.** A newly launched product is likely to need heavy advertising to inform customers of its existence and the benefits it provides. A well-known and established product may have sales promotions as a central element of its marketing mix to persuade customers to buy this product rather than those of its rivals.
- **The type of product.** Expensive products and those sold to businesses as well as those where design is a major element are likely to make greater use of exhibitions and trade fairs in the promotional mix. This element of the mix is important, for example, to firms selling homes, caravans, food and fashion products.
- **The finance available to the business.** Firms with larger budgets may engage more in public relations and personal selling, as these methods of promotion are expensive and may (especially in the case of PR) not provide results that are immediate or easily measurable.
- **Where consumers make purchasing decisions.** For businesses that sell products that consumers decide to buy on impulse, often at the point of sale, merchandising and packaging may be particularly important. The attractiveness of the wrappers and the positioning of the product within shops may be most important in these circumstances.
- **Competitors' actions.** If a business's rivals are engaging in a heavy campaign of advertising or extensive sales promotions, it is likely that the business will respond in a similar way. This reaction is more likely if the business trades in a market where there is relatively little product differentiation.

4 *Using the marketing mix: pricing*

What you need to know:
- the pricing strategies used by businesses
- the pricing tactics used by businesses
- influences on pricing decisions

4.1 The pricing strategies used by businesses

The **price** of a product is simply the amount that a business expects a customer to pay to purchase the good or service. For most products, price is determined in a free market by the forces of supply and demand.

Pricing strategies are the medium- to long-term pricing plans that a business adopts. There are four principal pricing strategies:
- **Price skimming.** Price skimming is often used when a new and innovative product is launched onto the market. It is unlikely that this product will face direct competition, at least in the short term. By setting a high price, the business will achieve a limited volume of sales but with a high profit margin on each sale. This will enable the firm to recoup some of the development costs of the product — with innovative products these might be high. The price is lowered when competitors enter the market.
- **Price leadership.** Price leadership is used for established products with strong brand images. The firm adopting this strategy will probably dominate the market and other businesses will usually follow their lead. It is common for price leaders to set their prices above the current market rate.
- **Penetration pricing.** Firms entering a market with products similar to those already available use penetration pricing. The price is set deliberately low to gain a foothold in the market. The expectation is that, once the product is established, the price will be increased to boost profits. Companies adopting this strategy rely on high sales to earn a reasonable level of profits.
- **Price taking.** Price takers set their prices equal to the 'going rate' or the established market price. This is a common pricing strategy for small and medium-sized businesses. Price takers have no influence over the market price, as they are normally one of many smallish forms competing for business. It is often the case that price takers sell similar products to those of competitors and this further reduces their ability to set prices independently. In the event of a price taker raising its price above the market price, it is likely to suffer a heavy fall in sales.

4.2 The pricing tactics used by businesses

Once a business has determined its medium- to long-term pricing strategy, it may employ a number of short-term pricing tactics. Pricing tactics are a series of pricing techniques that are normally used only over the short term to achieve specific goals. They include:
- **Loss leaders.** This entails setting prices very low (often below the cost of production) to attract customers. Businesses using this tactic hope that customers will purchase other (full-price) products while purchasing the loss leader. Supermarkets use this tactic extensively.
- **Special-offer pricing.** This approach involves reduced prices for a limited period of time or offers such as 'three for the price of two'.

- **Psychological pricing.** Many businesses set prices at £9.99 and £19.99 rather than £10 and £20, respectively. However, major retailers such as Marks and Spencer are using this tactic less frequently.

Examiner's tip

Don't confuse pricing strategies and pricing tactics. If a question asks about strategies, you must write about relevant pricing actions that a business can take in the long term, and not short-term tactical decisions that often cannot be sustained over a longer period.

4.3 Influences on pricing decisions

There is a range of factors that might influence a firm in its pricing decisions. A firm is more likely to select strategies and tactics that result in low prices if it is seeking to expand its market share. This type of approach may also be more popular with businesses that are in a financially strong position. In contrast, a business that is selling a product which is highly differentiated or facing increasing popularity may opt for strategies and tactics that lead to higher price levels.

Price elasticity of demand

One key factor influencing managers in their pricing decisions is **price elasticity of demand**. Price elasticity of demand measures the extent to which the level of demand for a product is sensitive to price changes. An increase in price is almost certain to reduce demand, while a price reduction can be expected to increase the level of demand. However, the extent to which demand changes following a given price change is less predictable.

Demand is said to be **price elastic** if it is sensitive to price changes. So, an increase in price will result in a significant lowering of demand and a fall in the firm's revenue. Products with a lot of competition (e.g. a brand of lager) are price elastic, as an increase in price will result in substantial numbers of consumers switching to rival products.

Price-inelastic demand exists when price changes have relatively little effect on the level of demand. Examples of products with price-inelastic demand are petrol, basic foodstuffs and other essentials. Products with few or no substitutes often have inelastic demand.

Price elasticity of demand (PED) is calculated by the formula:

$$PED = \frac{\text{percentage change in quantity demanded}}{\text{percentage change in price}}$$

For example, if a price rise of 5% leads to a fall in demand of 10%, PED = $-10/+5$ = -2. The figure that results is called the **coefficient of elasticity**.

The answers to PED calculations are always negative because there is always a negative figure in the calculation. If price rises, demand falls; and if price falls, demand rises.

If demand for a product is price inelastic, demand is not very responsive or sensitive to changes in price. In these circumstances, a price change will result in a smaller percentage change in quantity demanded. As a result, the coefficient of elasticity for a product in inelastic demand will be between 0 and –1. So products with elasticity coefficients of –0.25 or –0.6 will be in inelastic demand.

In contrast, a product with price-elastic demand will have a coefficient of elasticity somewhere between –1 and –∞. So a product with a value of –2 will have elastic demand.

The important thing about price elasticity of demand is that it determines how a price change will affect the business's **sales or total revenue**.

Examiner's tip

You will not be asked to calculate price elasticity of demand directly in an examination. It is much more likely that you will be given a price elasticity of demand figure for a product (which will be negative) and asked to comment on (or calculate) the effect of a given price change on the business's total revenue.

Firms calculate their sales revenue by multiplying the sales volume by the price at which they sell their products. Elasticity plays an important part in this calculation. For example, a firm facing price-inelastic demand would enjoy higher sales revenue if it raised its price. This is because the increase in price would have relatively little impact on the volume of sales. However, this would not be a wise approach in the case of price-elastic demand. In these circumstances, a price cut would be likely to lead to increased revenue, always assuming competitors did not cut their prices too (see Table 7.1).

	Price rise	Price cut
Elastic demand	Total revenue falls	Total revenue rises
Inelastic demand	Total revenue rises	Total revenue falls

Table 7.1 Price, elasticity and total revenue

Firms would prefer to sell products with demand that is price inelastic, as this gives greater freedom in selecting a pricing strategy and more opportunity to raise prices, total revenue and profits.

Businesses can adopt a number of techniques to make demand for their products more price inelastic:

- **Differentiating products from those of competitors.** Making a product significantly different from those available elsewhere on the market increases brand loyalty. Consumers are more likely to continue to purchase a product when its price rises if they can see that it has unique characteristics. Advertising is frequently used to differentiate products in the minds of consumers.
- **Reducing competition through takeovers and mergers.** In recent years, many markets have seen fewer, but larger firms competing with each other. For example, in 2005, chocolate manufacturer Cadbury bought its much smaller and organic competitor Green and Black's. Eventually, this process results in fewer products being available to the consumer. This means that demand will be less responsive to price, and firms will be able to take advantage of this.
- **Price fixing, which is alleged to take place in a number of markets.** Through the operation of a cartel, firms can agree 'standard' prices that reduce consumer choice and influence. This technique reduces the product's price elasticity, but is illegal in most countries.

5 *Using the marketing mix: place*

What you need to know:
- how businesses choose appropriate outlets and distributors
- the types of distribution channel that exist

The distribution of a good or service refers to the range of activities necessary to make the product available to customers.

5.1 How businesses choose appropriate outlets and distributors

As we will see in section 6, the choice of an outlet to sell the products or a distributor to supply the products to outlets must fit with the rest of the marketing mix. Therefore, it is vital that if the product is to be sold cheaply, possibly to increase market share, then suitable outlets are chosen. In this situation, a cost-cutting retail outlet might be appropriate, so that the benefit of low prices is passed on to the final customer.

In contrast, a business supplying a complex product that requires initial advice and ongoing support for customers would opt for outlets and distributors that had staff with the necessary skills and expertise. Businesses supplying computers might fall into this category.

Other factors that a business might take into account when choosing outlets and distributors include:
- **Location.** Businesses will seek outlets and distributors in areas where their target customers live and where few competitors operate.
- **Credit terms.** A small, newly established or struggling enterprise might opt for outlets or distributors that do not require long periods of trade credit. This can help to protect a business's cash-flow position.
- **Willingness to display products in prominent positions.** For some products (e.g. foods and confectionery), a good position in a retail outlet is an essential part of successful distribution.

5.2 The types of distribution channel that exist

There are a number of different forms of distribution. The three main channels are illustrated in Figure 7.6.

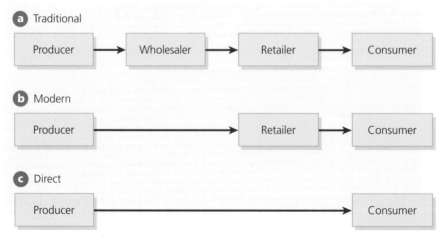

a Traditional

Producer → Wholesaler → Retailer → Consumer

b Modern

Producer → Retailer → Consumer

c Direct

Producer → Consumer

Figure 7.6 The channels of distribution

- **Traditional.** Many small retailers continue to purchase stock through wholesalers, as they do not purchase sufficient quantities to justify purchasing directly from producers. Wholesalers offer other benefits besides small quantities, such as advice, credit and delivery. However, the extra intermediary means that prices are inevitably higher, as the wholesaler's services do not come free.
- **Modern.** Major retailers such as Marks and Spencer and W. H. Smith do not purchase their products from a wholesaler. They purchase directly from manufacturers and arrange their own distribution. They can do this because they buy huge quantities of products and are able to negotiate large discounts that more than cover the costs of distribution. As a consequence, they can offer discounts to consumers, enhancing their market position. This approach is less common among smaller retailers.
- **Direct.** This is a rapidly growing channel of distribution. It is attractive to many firms because it lowers the prices at which they can sell products to the consumer. Firms selling direct avoid hefty overheads resulting from operating retail outlets. Many small businesses have started to sell their products directly to customers using the internet.

> **Examiner's tip**
>
> Don't ignore place or distribution. It is sometimes called 'the forgotten P' and students often respond poorly to questions that are set on it. You should know the different distribution methods and which are appropriate in different circumstances.

The choice of a distribution channel will be influenced by a number of factors:
- **The type of product.** Products that are difficult to transport due to their bulk, fragility or perishable nature are more likely to be distributed direct to avoid incurring additional costs. Producers selling large amounts of relatively low-priced products are more likely to use a wholesaler. It is expensive to store this type of product and producers will seek the opportunity to pass on these costs to others.
- **The nature of the market.** Markets that are widely dispersed or difficult to reach will usually require the services of wholesalers. Wholesalers have the facilities and expertise to deal effectively with this type of market.
- **The technical complexity of the product.** Technically complex products are better distributed when the customer and the producer can easily contact each other to solve problems of installation or operation. Computers are an example.

6 Designing an effective marketing mix

What you need to know:
- the influences on the marketing mix
- the importance of an integrated marketing mix

6.1 The influences on the marketing mix

Managers take a range of factors into account when designing the marketing mix for a product (see Figure 7.7).

Finance
The level of profits that a business earns can impact on the price that it charges. A profitable business is able to offer special terms to customers and to cut prices significantly, at least in the short term. Its financial reserves also enable it to engage in extensive promotional campaigns, including PR activities.

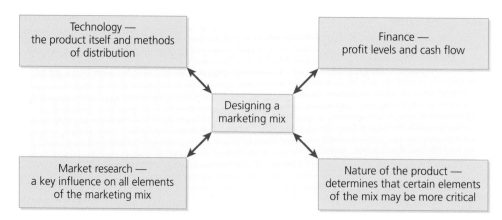

Figure 7.7 Influences on the marketing mix

Another aspect of finance that affects the marketing mix is that a business with a healthy cash flow will be able to extend the range of outlets and distributors it uses by offering favourable trade credit terms, or to fund special offers such as two for the price of one.

The nature of the product

The type of product can influence which elements of the mix are emphasised. An insurance firm may spend heavily on advertising because it is important to generate large numbers of enquiries in order to win an acceptable number of customers. In contrast, a portrait painter is much more likely to rely on the quality of the product and word-of-mouth to achieve his or her sales.

Technology

Some products that possess the latest technology may attract high levels of advertising to inform potential customers of their existence and benefits. The same products are also likely to operate with high prices to maximise short-term profits and cover the costs of research and development. Technology has also affected the place element of the marketing mix. Developments have allowed publishers of music and books to sell their products through internet downloads.

Market research

Arguably market research, and especially primary market research, is the most importance influence in the design of a marketing mix. The results of market research may provide information to help businesses to make judgements about the form, functions and design of the product, as respondents are likely to provide data on this aspect of the mix. It is also possible that research will uncover information on prices that consumers will be willing to pay and the type of people who are likely to buy the product. In these ways, market research may shape pricing strategies and the target audience at which advertising is aimed.

6.2 The importance of an integrated marketing mix

An **integrated marketing mix** is one that fits together. If a business is selling a premium product, the entire mix should support this. The elements might be constructed as follows:

- **Product.** This should be high quality in terms of design, innovativeness, features or functions.
- **Price.** The price is likely to be high (skimming) to reflect the premium nature of the product.

- **Place.** The business would seek outlets that reflected the quality or exclusiveness of the product.
- **Promotion.** This would be targeted at the people who are likely to purchase the product (e.g. relatively wealthy individuals) and carry the required premium image.

If the marketing mix is inconsistent in any way, this may deter some consumers from purchasing the product, thereby depressing sales and profits. In the case of a premium product, a low price might be a mistake as it may lead some consumers to believe that the product is not of premium quality.

7 Marketing and competitiveness

What you need to know:
- the impact of market conditions and the degree of competition
- the determinants of competitiveness
- methods of improving competitiveness

7.1 The impact of market conditions and the degree of competition

Market structure

There are a number of ways of judging a market. We can consider its size or growth rate as we saw earlier in this book. We can also consider the **structure** of the market and the way in which it influences the marketing behaviour of a business. The structure of a market takes into account two factors:

- **The number of businesses in the market.** If a business faces a greater number of competitors, it is likely to face tough competition. This statement is more likely to be true if the business faces a lot of nearby competitors that sell products which are similar, and if they are able to sell their products at similar prices. A small town with a number of estate agents offering the same services would be considered a competitive market and this might be reflected in the way the estate agents market themselves. They might spend heavily on promotion, focus on providing top-quality service and be prepared to negotiate on prices.
- **The relative size and power of the businesses.** It is not uncommon for small and medium-sized business to face much larger competitors. For example, in the UK banking market, relatively small building societies (e.g. the Buckinghamshire Building Society with two branches) compete with multinational finance businesses such as HSBC. In such circumstances, smaller enterprises may be unable to compete in terms of price or advertising. For small businesses facing larger and more powerful rivals, the product itself and the associated quality of service may be highly important elements.

Barriers to entry

The structure of the market can influence the marketing actions taken by a business in other ways. An established business with a degree of market power (in terms of profits or market share) may take actions to prevent new rivals entering the market. Such actions are designed to establish **barriers to entry** and prevent or restrict free entry by firms to a given market. Barriers include:

- **Establishing and extending brand loyalty.** Brand-loyal customers are happy to make repeat purchases from a business. This can be encouraged by offering discounts to regular customers or by giving customers long-term benefits through loyalty card schemes.

- **Seeking legal restrictions.** Many businesses may seek to obtain patents on products or processes that they produce. Although a patent only operates for a given period, this can prevent other businesses from supplying similar products.

Some barriers exist because of the nature of the business and help existing suppliers to protect their market power by maintaining the given market structure. The most common is the existence of **high entry costs**. A business seeking to enter the car manufacturing market could be prevented from doing so by high start-up costs. A business wishing to enter this market would need to purchase expensive assets such as factories and production machinery as well as spending heavily on marketing.

It is logical for businesses to seek to erect and maintain barriers to protect their market share. They may do this by introducing new brands to dilute the effect of a new supplier entering the market. They may spend heavily on marketing to increase the entry costs of potential market entrants. They may also supply at low prices to deter new entrants by reducing potential profitability.

7.2 The determinants of competitiveness

Competitiveness is the extent to which a firm is successful in outperforming its rivals in the marketplace. Competitiveness can take a number of forms.

Price competitiveness

A price competitive firm is able to provide a product to its customers at a lower price than its rivals. However, this alone is not sufficient to provide a competitive advantage. The benefits provided by the product must also at least equal those of its rivals. A highly price competitive firm would provide a product with superior benefits at a lower price: easyCar and easyCinema have promoted themselves on the basis of price competitiveness.

Product competitiveness

This form of competitiveness is based on the benefits provided by a product. If a business provides a higher-quality good or enhanced levels of customer service, the consumer will receive greater benefits and may prefer the product to those supplied by its rivals. In these circumstances, customers will be willing to pay higher prices for the product. However, the price differential should not outweigh the additional benefits provided by the product in the eyes of the consumer. Farmers supplying organic products may be considered to be product competitive.

Competitiveness through image

Some businesses spend heavily on promotion to build up an image for the business or product that is attractive to its target audience. Some companies that supply fashion clothing pay celebrities large sums of money to promote their products to increase their desirability. Other businesses have concentrated on developing an environmentally friendly image as a means of creating a strong competitive position.

Developing a unique selling point

By having a particular feature or function that makes its product different from other companies' products, the business may be able to win customers from its rivals. This form of competitiveness is especially valuable if the USP can be protected by a patent or copyright.

A firm that has a competitive advantage should not assume that it will maintain this advantage in the longer term. It will need to take action to do so. Changes in technology or in consumers' tastes and fashions can mean that a competitive advantage slips away. Managers have to be alert to this, monitor changes in the market and be prepared to change their approach to marketing to maintain their position.

7.3 Methods of improving competitiveness

A business can improve its competitiveness by working on any of the forms of competitiveness outlined in the previous section.

Improving price competitiveness

Managers can use a number of techniques to improve the price competitiveness of their businesses. In essence, these rely upon reducing the costs of production:

- Increasing the productivity of the workforce (possibly through training schemes or improving job design) to reduce the labour cost of producing the good or service.
- Using less of more expensive resources (possibly labour) and more of cheaper resources (possibly capital) in the production process.
- Seeking cheaper sources of supplies of raw materials and components without compromising quality.
- Reducing the number of substandard products or services to reduce 'wasted' expenditure.

Improving product competitiveness

Businesses often advertise 'new, improved' products. What does this mean? The business in question may have reduced the size of a product such as a laptop, or given its mobile phone more functions, or increased the quality of customer service associated with the product. The nature of product competitiveness will vary according to the nature of the product. A restaurant may improve product competitiveness by offering organic ingredients or expert advice on choosing wines. A public house might decide to open for longer hours, while a house builder could improve the specifications of its properties.

Improving image competitiveness

A business can cultivate a more positive image among its potential customers by:

- being seen to protect the environment through operating recycling schemes, using sustainable resources, minimising carbon emissions and disposing of its waste products responsibly
- treating its employees fairly and with respect, offering ongoing training and opportunities for promotion and personal development
- contributing to community schemes such as clearing up litter, financing youth clubs and allowing local communities to use its facilities

Developing a unique selling point

Anything that differentiates a business and its products from the others in the market can form the basis of competitive advantage. The quality of customer service may be important to businesses that are supplying services. This could be achieving by investing regularly in staff training or operating an effective recruitment system to employ the best-quality employees possible. For many manufacturing businesses, a USP might be created by supplying products with features or functions that rival products do not possess, or designing products to meet the demands of individual customers precisely.

1 General advice in preparing for Unit 2

1.1 The examination

The examination will comprise two data-response questions that will cover the internal functions of businesses. The two questions will relate to two different businesses, one of which is likely to be a real business. The two businesses will be small or medium-sized organisations.

Each of the data-response scenarios will have approximately four questions based on it and the questions will cover a range of internal functions that operate within businesses. Key facts relating to this examination are as follows:

- Duration: 1 hour and 30 minutes.
- Total marks available: 80.
- Each of the four functions will have questions worth roughly (but not necessarily exactly) 20 marks.
- Weighting of the examination: 60% of AS; 30% of A-level.
- Available: January and June from January 2009.

Unit 2 considers small to medium-sized enterprises. The focus of this unit is to consider how the managers of such businesses might use functional and tactical techniques (e.g. altering the marketing mix, recruiting new employees or training existing staff, and increasing capacity utilisation) to improve the performance of the business.

The unit also covers how managers can measure the performance of various functions of the business. For example, the performance of the workforce might be measured by labour productivity and the operation's function through the level of capacity utilisation. It is important for you to be able to carry out relevant calculations and to interpret the results.

A copy of AQA's specimen Unit 2 paper and the marking scheme can be found on the following webpage:

www.aqa.org.uk/qual/gce/pdf/business_studies_new.php

1.2 How to prepare for the Unit 2 examination

This examination requires you to have mastered all of the material that comprises Unit 2 — **knowledge** is essential. The questions on the paper will be wide ranging and the papers are constructed to test all of the relevant areas of the specification. So the starting point of your preparation must be to master all the relevant material. Without offering relevant knowledge in your answers to any of the Unit 2 questions, you will be unable to score marks for any of the other skills.

It is important to learn the relevant definitions, as these provide a sound starting point for most answers. In the same way, it is sensible to make sure you know all the relevant formulae for financial and other calculations.

However, this examination tests other skills too. As shown in Table 8.1, they carry 79% of the marks on this paper.

Skill	Marks	%
Knowledge	21	26.7
Application	19	23.3
Analysis	23	28.3
Evaluation	17	21.7
Total	80	100

Table 8.1 Mark allocations for Unit 2

Application

Application is the skill of applying your answers to the context set out in the examination paper. This is an important skill in Unit 2. Each of the data-response questions will provide you with information about a particular business and a fair proportion of this information is likely to be in the form of numbers. It is essential that you relate your answers to these businesses and avoid writing general theoretical answers. The examiner will include hooks for you to use in developing your responses — these may be numerical in form. He or she may say that the business faces rising unit costs, is uncompetitive or suffers from high turnover of labour. These are things that you can use in your answers to help to gain application marks.

Analysis

Analysis is developing a line of argument and following it through. This skill carries the highest proportion of marks on this paper (over 28%). Analysis commonly focuses on causes or effects or on interrelationships. Do think about the theories that you have studied in this unit and consider how they can be used to help businesses to improve their performance. You will remember from answering questions on Unit 1 that questions requiring analysis use verbs (or command words) such as 'analyse' and 'examine'.

Evaluation

This is the skill of judgement. Questions on Unit 2 calling for evaluation carry high mark allocations (approximately between 10 and 15 marks). You can recognise this type of question by command words such as 'discuss', 'evaluate', 'to what extent' and 'justify'. Good evaluation often builds on the skill of application by making judgements about the specific business, rather than businesses in general. Good evaluation makes a clear judgement and supports it.

2 *A sample Unit 2 examination paper*

Question 1: Watson's of Cambridge

Watson's of Cambridge is a supplier of conservatories in the east of England. It offers a one-stop service from design to construction and has an excellent reputation for individual designs in keeping with the property and location. Watson's promotes itself as a builder of quality products and benefits from price-inelastic demand.

The company built 506 conservatories in 2008, slightly fewer than in the previous year, but with a significant increase in its average selling price. The company's profits have risen steadily in recent years and reached a record level of £3.6 million in 2007/08.

Watson's trades in a competitive market but succeeds in part due to its coordinated marketing mix. The company charges relatively high prices (5–10% more than its leading rivals) for its products. The management team protects the company's image as a supplier of top-quality conservatories and incorporates the latest technology in its designs. Watson's customers have high incomes and are drawn mainly from the ABC1 market research classifications. The company uses market research regularly to confirm that its products meet with customers' needs and expectations.

Watson's selects its suppliers carefully with a particular emphasis on quality of materials. In addition the management team at Watson's expect suppliers to be reliable and to deliver on time. This is vital if the company is to maintain its reputation as a quality supplier. Watson's rarely changes its suppliers of glass, doors, windows and other materials, and has traded with many for 20 years.

The company's managers place great value on its workforce. Watson's operates an effective system of recruitment and selection to help maintain its performance. The level of labour turnover is low and the company invests heavily in technical training and also in developing high levels of customer service skills. Once recruited and suitably trained, Watson's employees work as part of empowered teams responsible for various aspects of the company's operations. As a result, the company's organisational structure contains few levels of hierarchy, encouraging effective communication between all staff.

Questions

(a) Explain fully what is meant by the term 'price-inelastic demand'. (4 marks)

(b) Analyse the importance of 'an effective system of recruitment and selection' to the performance of Watson's labour force. (9 marks)

(c) To what extent is Watson's success dependent on its choice of suppliers? (12 marks)

(d) Do you consider that market research is the major influence on the design of Watson's marketing mix? Justify your view. (15 marks)

Total for question 1: 40 marks

Question 2: Roberto's Pizzas

Roberto Maldini operates a chain of seven pizza restaurants in London. The restaurants are popular in the summer months when London is crowded with tourists, although some of the locations are away from major thoroughfares. Roberto has enjoyed managing a rapidly growing business — four new restaurants have been opened in the last 18 months. However, his fellow shareholders have been disappointed with their returns and also by the fact that the restaurant chain has suffered from cash-flow problems on occasions.

Roberto has sometimes delayed payment to suppliers and, as a consequence, is offered little if any trade credit. He insists on buying high-quality ingredients although, because the restaurant market is very competitive, he cannot always charge prices that reflect his costs. He does, however, take pride in the fact that the company has purchased a number of the properties that it uses as restaurants.

Although most of his restaurants make a positive contribution to overheads, Roberto is concerned that some are significantly less profitable than others. The overheads on most restaurants are high and the competitive nature of the market means that contribution levels are relatively low. The Leicester Square branch is underperforming in terms of profits when judged against Roberto's expectations.

Roberto has had lengthy discussions with the manager of this restaurant, which has relatively low numbers of customers, even at peak times. On some evenings, many of its tables are unoccupied and staff are not as busy as they should be. Roberto is concerned that his employees, including managers, are less motivated than he would wish. He is unsure whether to offer financial incentives or to offer employees greater empowerment by giving them more control over their working lives.

Roberto's Pizzas — Leicester Square Branch

	May Budget (£)	May Actual (£)	June Budget (£)	June Actual (£)	July Budget (£)	July Actual (£)
Sales of pizzas	4,500	3,000	5,200	4,100	7,200	6,000
Sales of drinks	3,200	2,200	4,100	3,000	5,500	4,500
Sales revenue	7,700	5,200	9,300	7,100	12,700	10,500
Materials	950	660	1,050	900	1,500	1,500
Rent and rates	3,500	3,500	3,500	3,450	3,500	3,500
Salaries	1,500	1,500	1,500	1,500	1,500	1,500
Costs	5,950	5,660	6,050	5,850	6,500	6,500
Profit/(loss)	1,750	(460)	3,250	1,250	6,200	4,000

Questions

(a) (i)   Identify two examples of favourable variances from the table above.   (2 marks)

   (ii) Use the table above to calculate the profit variance for Leicester Square for the 3 months from May to July.   (6 marks)

(b) Examine why achieving high levels of capacity utilisation might be important to Roberto's business.   (9 marks)

(c) Evaluate the possible ways in which Roberto might improve his business's cash-flow position.   (11 marks)

(d) Would Roberto be better advised to use financial methods or employee empowerment to improve the motivation of his workforce? Justify your view.   (12 marks)

Total for question 2: 40 marks